Engaged in Battle

Engaged in Battle

Davo Roberts

Acknowledgements

Engaged in Battle – version 1.0

Text & Graphics Copyright © 2022 Dave G Roberts

ISBN–13: 9798351289663

Also available:
Kindle
Paperback (ISBN: 9781508657200)

Parts of this publication have previously been released as Podcasts on the Partakers website: http://www.partakers.co.uk

Parts of this publication may also have been published in other PulpTheology Publications

No part of this publication may be reproduced or transmitted in any form or by any means, electronic or mechanical, including photocopy, recording, or any information storage and retrieval system, without express written permission in writing from the author(s).

All Scripture quotations, unless otherwise indicated, are taken from the Holy Bible, New International Version®, NIV®. Copyright ©1973, 1978, 1984, 2011 by Biblica, Inc.™ Used by permission of Zondervan. All rights reserved worldwide. www.zondervan.com The "NIV" and "New International Version" are trademarks registered in the United States Patent and Trademark Office by Biblica, Inc.™

Dedication

To the Lord our God – Father, Son and Holy Spirit. I wouldn't be here without Him.

My wife, Youngmi. She is my one and my only. I can't imagine life without her and I thank God for her daily.

Roger Kirby, who was mentor, editor, but most of all, good friend. He fought the good fight and is now in the presence of His Saviour, Jesus Christ.

Karen, a friend from High School, who was the first person to invite me to a Church, Noosa Baptist Church, where I heard the Gospel for the first time and responded with a yes.

Lastly, to the thousands of listeners globally of our Podcasts and YouTube videos. Thanks for your silent encouragements.

How To Look Up The Bible

The following diagram will help you if you are not used to reading the Bible.

Contents

Dedication v
How To Look Up The Bible vii

Introduction 11
Section A: Adversary Awareness 15
   A1. Satan 16
   A2. Sin And Old Nature 24
   A3. The World 34
Section B: The Armour We Wear 42
   B1. Belt of Truth 46
   B2. Breastplate of Righteousness 52
   B3. Gospel Feet 58
   B4. Shield of Faith 66
   B5. Helmet of Salvation 72
   B6. Sword of the Spirit 80
Section C: Weapon of Memory 86
   C1. We March In God's Victory 87
   C2. We Abide With God 94
   C3. We Are God's Children 102
   C4. We Converse With God 110
   C5. We Keep On Learning About God 118
   C6. We Live Out Joy 124
   C7. We Persevere and Overcome 132
   C8. We Remain Committed 142
   C9. We Will Be With Others 152
   C10. We Worship God Only 162

A Final Word 171
Becoming a Christian 174

Chief Abbreviations 176
Index of Bible References 178

Other PulpTheology Publications 178
About Partakers 189

Introduction

[15] The Son is the image of the invisible God, the firstborn over all creation. [16] For in Him all things were created: things in heaven and on earth, visible and invisible, whether thrones or powers or rulers or authorities; all things have been created through Him and for Him. [17] He is before all things, and in Him all things hold together. [18] And He is the head of the body, the Church; He is the beginning and the firstborn from among the dead, so that in everything He might have the supremacy. [19] For God was pleased to have all His fullness dwell in Him, [20] and through Him to reconcile to Himself all things, whether things on earth or things in heaven, by making peace through His blood, shed on the cross. (Colossians 1:15–20)

Here is a brief word picture from the Apostle Paul concerning Jesus Christ, the Son of God. This word picture includes Jesus' divinity, humanity, birth, life, death, resurrection, supremacy, power and authority. This word picture continues with Jesus being seen as eternal, creator, leader, sustainer, reconciler, peace–maker and peace–giver. That is the majesty of Jesus Christ, whom. I have willingly followed Him for about forty years since He first called me, to follow Him.

Yet in human form, during His earthly ministry, Jesus had no physical beauty that would draw people naturally to Himself. Jesus' body on the cross was disfigured and tortured beyond that of human likeness. His perfect life, salvation work on the cross and His subsequent rising from the dead, is what makes Jesus Christ unique. Jesus is the once and for all Messiah or Saviour for the entire world. The great God of creation, stepping into His creation as a human, with the purpose of reconciling the world back to Himself. Jesus' uniqueness entails that I can participate in having an active, intimate and dynamic personal relationship with God Almighty.

Jesus Christ is replete with majesty and awe! He is not simply a king with a crown upon His head. He is the King of Kings and the Lord of Lords! There is no other like Him! What's more, this Jesus Christ did not decay in the grave. By no means no! He overcame death in the grave and was raised again majestically to new life! As Paul said about Jesus' resurrection, that Jesus is "the firstborn from among the dead" (Colossians 1:18).

Jesus Christ is the King of all Kings and Lord of all Lords, who with unparalleled majesty, is the head of His body, the Church (Colossians 1:18), which is God's orchestra of joy. If Jesus did not rise from the dead, the Church would not be in existence two thousand years later, let alone two years after His death. Jesus' majesty signifies that I can depend upon Him for all matters of life. When I look into the eyes of Jesus, I see His tenderness and compassion. Jesus looks upon people with love, adoration, justice and tenderness. Eyes that are filled with mercy, grace, love and compassion. Eyes that fill with rage at injustice and oppression! His penetrating eyes that can separate flesh and spirit! This Jesus is kind, compassionate and sympathetic. His look of love on a world that is separated from God, and a world that He is calling back into an actively intimate relationship with God. Jesus' tenderness meaning that I can run to Him for comfort because He sees and understands all that I go through.

When Jesus spoke words, people were amazed! They were astounded that He spoke with elegance and yet with authority (Matthew 7:29). They had never heard anyone speak like He did – with both grace and authority. The same is true today. That is why I read the Bible to find out what He would say to me. That is why I seek to hear Him speak to me and why I speak to Him. Jesus' wisdom, signifying that I can ask Him for advice about all facets of life and seek His wise imagination to solve burdens and problems that I throw His way in prayer. Jesus is strong enough and capable enough, to carry any burden that I may lay upon Him.

Introduction

Jesus Christ gives a solid and sure foundation for all aspects of my life. A solid foundation which will never fall or be destroyed. Indeed, Jesus Christ will and can never fall or decay such is His imperishability as the everlasting Son of God. Jesus Christ is solid, dependable and strong. Because of Jesus' strength, I can go to Him for protection and strength when I am weak, knowing that He will supply my needs and take care of me. Jesus is beyond compare for the things He has done and the things He will do. Jesus Christ is altogether lovely in regard to His person, humanity, birth, life, ministry, death, resurrection, ascension, exultation, glorification, grace, protection, tenderness, power, wisdom, vengeance, judgment, majesty, redemption and pardon! Jesus' loveliness means I can have His incomparable joy when I feel defeated and dejected.

That is my Jesus: unique, majestic, tender, wise, strong, and lovely. That is my Jesus, whom I seek to serve and obey in every facet of life, every second of every day. I rarely ever fully achieve it, but I know that when I fail, I can ask for forgiveness, and He will grant it from His abundant wellsprings of grace and mercy. It is this Jesus whom I depend upon and personally know to be reliable in every way. All through each day, I know that Jesus is dependable, going ahead of me and with me! Amazing!

As a Christian, I am in an active, intimate and passionate relationship with Almighty God. As are you, if you are a Christian. Because we are Christians, we are sojourners travelling together. We are in a spiritual battle. Who or what is this battle against? What protection and weapons do we have for this battle? Let's go!

Section A: Adversary Awareness

As Christians, we are commanded to be strong in the Lord against our enemies, all those who would come against us in the spiritual battle we are in (Ephesians 6:10). But who are these enemies who oppose us and engage us in this spiritual battle? They are sin and our old nature, as well as the world, who are raising their heads against us as Christians. But behind these adversaries, is the unseen enemy in the spiritual realm, the devil.

Come and let's discover what the Bible has to say concerning our adversaries, what Jesus Christ has already done, is still doing in our lives as Christians, as well as how we as Christians are armoured and weaponized against our adversaries.

A1. Satan

Satan, the devil, is the arch slanderer. He is real, he is personal and he is a threat. We can forget the lampooning caricatures such as the cute little red figure with two horns on his head, often perpetrated in modern media.

Historically, as well as today, parts of the Church have made errors concerning Satan. They have either encouraged blind ignorance about Satan or they have given him far more importance, credence and privilege than he deserves or warrants. There are many people today, including inside the Church, who think that Satan is not real and can therefore be no real threat. However, Satan is real. Jesus spoke about Satan more than anyone else did. Indeed, Jesus Christ Himself had His own dealings with Satan.

What are the origins of Satan? Some angels rebelled against God and were put out of heaven (Isaiah 14:12–15; Luke 10:18; 2 Peter 2:4; Jude 6). When Satan sinned against God, he was expelled from Heaven (Revelation 12:9), although evidently, he still had some access to God (Job 1:6). He is the great accuser against God's people. A multitude of angels decided to follow him in his fall and later became what are called the demons (Matthew 12:24; Revelation 12:7). Satan is their leader and he has established his kingdom here on earth. The role of Satan against the Christian is summed up by his various names: devil, accuser, angel of light, and the arch–deceiver.

As these names suggest, he stands hatefully opposed to all God's work and God's people – including you and me. He resourcefully promotes defiance among all peoples and attacks God's people in many subtle and varied ways (Job 2:4–5; Mark 4:15). Although Satan's doom was secured by Jesus' death on the cross (John 16:11), he continues to try and hinder God's program. But one day, Satan and his demons will finally be obliterated by being cast into the lake of fire (Revelation 20:10).

Section A. Adversary Awareness

Satan is described as controlling the whole world (1 John 5:19). He is also known as the devil (Matthew 13:39) and the God of this age (2 Corinthians 4:4). He exerts himself and his will, all the while masquerading as an angel of light and his servants masquerade as angels of righteousness (2 Corinthians 11:14–15). Satan is known as the prince of this world (John 14:30), the ruler of the kingdom of the air (Ephesians 2:2) and the authority and power of this dark world (Ephesians 6:12). He is the wicked one who snatches away the good seed (Matthew 13:19) and always sows bad seed (Matthew 13:39).

He is also known by other descriptive names such as the adversary (the meaning of the name 'Satan'), the destroyer who devours (1 Peter 5:8), the destroyer by disease (Luke 13:11, 16), the accuser of the family of God (Revelation 12:10) and the holder of the power of death (Hebrews 2:14). Satan is the ultimate liar, the father of all lies, who is described as a murderer (John 8:44), schemer (2 Corinthians 2:11; Ephesians 6:11) and tempter (1 Thessalonians 3:5).

If that is who Satan is, what does Satan do in regard to Christian believers? Satan goes around like a hunting lion (1 Peter 5:8) who attacks (Ephesians 6:16) and sifts (Luke 22:31) Christians. Satan tries to lure, deceive and lead God's people astray with wrong and demonic thinking (2 Corinthians 11:3; 1 Timothy 4:1; James 3:15). Where there is discord between Christians, you can be sure Satan is in the middle of that discord. Satan hates everything to do with God, including the Church. It is Satan who tries to cause Christians to have doubt, uncertainty, confusion, fear, stress and darkness. These are Satan's fruit, the outworking of all that he is. Satan tempts us to sin against God, other people and ourselves (1 Thessalonians 3:5). Satan does all this because he wants us to compromise our faith in God. He wants us to be fearful, to have doubts and blasphemous thoughts. He wants us to be hedonists who only think of ourselves and to live a materialistic life which is only pleasing to ourselves. He wants us to be an isolated individual, instead of being involved in our local Christian community.

Satan is not alone, however. He cannot be in more than one place at once. He may be powerful, but he is neither almighty nor omnipresent. He has helpers that are called demons, who fell with Satan during the angelic rebellion against God. These demons, or fallen angels, are called wicked (Matthew 12:45) and evil (Acts 19:13). They know about Jesus and His authority, and they also know their eternal fate is destruction and torment (Matthew 8:29–31).

Because of this, they want to take as many humans with them as possible. Consequently, they tempt humans to disobey God (Genesis 3) and also possess people (Mark 5:1–20). Furthermore, we know that if we haven't recently met opposition from Satan and his minions, it may just be that we are probably going the way that he wants us to, and therefore, we pose no hindrance to him and his schemes. So, what can we do? How can we resist his attacks?

Firstly, we are not left alone to our own devices and means.

[13] To which of the angels did God ever say,

'Sit at my right hand until I make your enemies a footstool for your feet'?

[14] Are not all angels ministering spirits sent to serve those who will inherit salvation? (Hebrews 1:13–14)

We may also have angelic help. Angels are mentioned frequently in the Bible; at least 100 times in the Old Testament and 175 times in the New Testament. They are created beings (Psalm 148:2–5) and were possibly created before humanity (Job 38:7). These spiritual beings, angels, also serve humans who are inheriting salvation (Hebrews 1:14). They do not die (Luke 20:36), and they do not marry (Mark 12:25). Angels are personal, intelligent and able to communicate with humans. They have a will (2 Peter 2:4), are separate from humanity (1 Corinthians 6:3) and they are powerful yet also finite. There are large companies of angels (Revelation 5:11), and they do not naturally increase unless God creates more. They are organized and there are ranks of angels. For example,

Section A. Adversary Awareness

there is Michael the archangel (Jude 9) and there are legions of angels (Matthew 26:53). Cherubim are another class of angel. Their job was to protect (Genesis 3:24) and their likenesses were also seen on the Ark of the Covenant (Exodus 25:17–22) presumably to indicate their real but unseen presence.

As the Greek word *'angelos'* means 'messenger', they carry God's messages. Such as at the prediction of the coming of John the Baptist (Luke 1:11–20). For Elijah, they provided food (1 Kings 19:5–8), whereas for Daniel, they protected him from the lions (Daniel 6:22) and angels ministered to Jesus after His temptations in the wilderness (Matthew 4:11).

We also know that angels are holy (Matthew 18:10; Mark 8:38), and that they praise and worship God with all their being (Psalm 89:7). This is seen in their rejoicing at God's work (Revelation 5:11–12), their rejoicing at the birth of Jesus (Luke 2:13–14) and their rejoicing at a sinner's conversion (Luke 15:10). Angels watch over Christians (Hebrews 1:14) and they carry out God's judgments (2 Kings 19:35; Matthew 16:27). The prophet Daniel intimates that angels also guide nations (Daniel 10–12). The Apostle John, writing what God commanded of him, seems to indicate that Churches have angels to watch over them (Revelation 2–3).

Now an obvious question. How can we know the difference between God's good, holy angels and Satan and his demons, the fallen angels? We listen to what they are telling us. If what they say is bringing all glory to God, then they are truly from God. Why? Because in all the Biblical accounts, angels from God always give the glory and honour directly to God. If they don't, then they cannot be from God. However, the job of spreading the Gospel is not for angels. It is for Christians to do so, as commanded by Jesus (Matthew 28:18–20). God obviously thinks that way is a much more efficient and effective method, than getting angels to do it. If we were to see an angel, how would we react? Would we be afraid, as the women at Jesus' tomb seemingly were when the angel told them about Jesus having risen from the dead (Matthew 28:5)? Would we bow to worship them just as the Apostle John endeavoured to do, before the angel rebuked him and stopped him from doing so?

> "But he said to me, 'Don't do that! I am a fellow servant with you and with your fellow prophets and with all who keep the words of this scroll. Worship God!'" (Revelation 22:9)

I know from these and other Bible stories that humans have seen angels, albeit rarely. Jacob did so when on his way to meet Esau (Genesis 32:1) as did those who witnessed Jesus' ascension (Acts 1:10). As angels are God's messengers, they must be listened to as well as be allowed to serve and to minister to us. By practising hospitality, particularly to those we don't know, we may well be unaware that we are entertaining angels (Hebrews 13:2). We know that angels are not to be worshipped, both according to Paul (Colossians 2:18) and to angels themselves (Revelation 22:8–9). Also, according to Paul, we will be judging angels (1 Corinthians 6:3). Have we have indeed been ministered to by angels or indeed ministered to angels, and yet been unaware of it?

Secondly, we can remind ourselves that Satan is defeated and beaten. God's Son, Jesus Christ, came to destroy Satan and his works (1 John 3:8). This was done through Jesus Christ's death on the cross, which leads to Satan's destruction (Hebrews 2:14). Satan has been disarmed (Colossians 2:15), defeated and condemned (Matthew 25:41). As Christians, we are in Jesus Christ; therefore, we are protected under God's mighty hand.

Nobody, including Satan despite his threats, can snatch us from under the protective hand of God (John 10:28–29). Jesus Christ is infinitely superior to Satan (1 John 4:4; 1 John 5:18), because Jesus is fully God and Satan is a mere created being. We are to resist Satan and his schemes, commands Peter, therefore we are to be steadfast in the faith (1 Peter 5:9). James reminds us, that Satan will leave as we resist

Section A. Adversary Awareness

him by submitting and giving ourselves solely to God alone (James 4:7). We are not to give Satan any opportunity to gain a foothold in our life through things such as "bitterness, rage and anger, brawling and slander, along with every form of malice" (Ephesians 4:31).

Because of Jesus, Satan is nothing more than an annoying nuisance to us. Despite his lies and promises, Satan cannot take anything from us, particularly our salvation and God's love of us. We are also to take note and not blame Satan for our own sin. He may tempt us, but we commit the sin, transgressing against God, other people and our own self. We are not to believe the lies he tells us in our head. When we have sinned, we often hear a little voice in our head saying: "You are a failure now. God won't forgive you again. Why don't you just give up on God and being one of His so called children."

These are lies and we are not to believe them as Satan attempts to undermine and discourage us. Yet we know the truth is, that if we confess our sins to God in penitence and faith, then God from His wellsprings of grace and mercy, will forgive us (1 John 1:9). We are to rely on the authority of God's Word just as Jesus did (Matthew 4:1–11). Satan is a defeated creature. We know that, because he was defeated when Jesus, the Son of God, went to His death on the cross and rose again to new life three days later.

Becoming a Christian is the best thing that has happened to us. Certainly for me. Despite what Satan may tell us to the contrary. We have the victory because God the Holy Spirit comes to indwell us as Christians, sealing us as a beloved child of God and as part of God's family. We can also be assured that we can overcome and persevere because as Jesus said:

> [4] "You, dear children, are from God and have overcome them, because the one who is in you is greater than the one who is in the world. [5] They are from the world and therefore speak from the viewpoint of the world, and the world listens to them."
> (1 John 4:4–5)

Satan and his minions were defeated by Jesus Christ, and they are defeated creatures. God has decreed the destiny of Satan and his demons, who will be spending eternity in a place called 'hell' (Matthew 25:41; 2 Peter 2:4). This is a place described as being completely god-less, which is a place of everlasting fire and punishment (Matthew 25:41–46) with a constant and outer darkness (Matthew 8:12), which leads to everlasting destruction (2 Thessalonians 1:9) amid lakes of fire (Revelation 19:20). This punishment is to be physical (Matthew 5:29–30) and of the soul (Matthew 10:28).

However, this place is not just for Satan and his demons but is also for all people who are declared by God to be the wicked (Revelation 21:8) and disobedient (Romans 2:8–9). This includes those who reject Jesus Christ and His Gospel (Matthew 10:14–15) and whose names who are not written in the Book of Life (Revelation 13:8; Revelation 20:12). Finally, it is also for somebody declared to be the 'Beast', for his worshippers and the false prophet (Revelation 14:11; Revelation 19:20). All of this is very alarming if we really stop to think about it. We all know plenty of nice people who are close to us, whose "names have not been written in the Lamb's book of life, the Lamb who was slain from the creation of the world." (Revelation 13:8). Then there are millions, probably billions, of people in this world who have never heard of Jesus Christ or have only ever heard very distorted views of who He was, is or what He has done. These people don't have the assurance of salvation through Jesus Christ that we have. Do we really think they will all end up in hell? As Christians, it increases the imperative for us to continue growing as a follower of Jesus. Not only that but we are also to go and tell the good news about living for Jesus and having eternity with Him, in a place called paradise or 'heaven', so that hell is not a person's final destination. We may just be the only person they meet who can tell them the wonderful news of the Gospel.

However, as intimated earlier, Satan and his minions, are not alone in having engaged battle against those who are Christians.

Section A. Adversary Awareness

Encouragement From Other Sojourners

We were ensnared by the wisdom of the serpent: we are set free by the foolishness of God. Moreover, just as the former was called wisdom, but was in reality the folly of those who despised God, so the latter is called foolishness, but is true wisdom in those who overcome the devil.[1]

One of Satan's deadliest weapons is to attack believers with doubts about whether they are among the elect, and then incite them to look for answers in the wrong way.[2]

It is no wonder that Satan is an enemy to Christ, His people and kingdom, and sets himself against Jesus with all his power and cunning. 'Tis an old hate and grudge between them, which began in Paradise. They are, by nature and kind, of contrary mind and dispositions.[3]

He who will have for His master and king, Jesus Christ, the son of the Virgin, who took upon Himself our flesh and our blood, will have the devil for His enemy.[4]

The devil's aim is to shift us from the terrain of trusting God. In the heat of the battle then, we are to dig our heels in, not yielding ground taken so far.[5]

---

[1] Augustine, Page 25
[2] Calvin, Page 219
[3] Luther, Page 137
[4] Luther, Page 351
[5] Whitman, Page 182

A2. Sin And Old Nature

I once had a favourite jacket. I would wear it everywhere because it was so comfortable and cosy. Then one day, I realised that this jacket was dirty and smelled badly. It was filthy and needed washing. It was no longer fit to be worn yet I still wanted to wear it because it was familiar to me and comfortable. But I couldn't wear it because it was only fit for being put in the rubbish bin. So that is where it ended up.

That is the similar for all those of us who are Christians, in regard to the old sinful nature with which we were physically born. Paul uses this imagery when he writes :

> "[22] You were taught, with regard to your former way of life, to put off your old self, which is being corrupted by its deceitful desires; [23] to be made new in the attitude of your minds; [24] and to put on the new self, created to be like God in true righteousness and holiness." (Ephesians 4:22–24)

This old self, or old nature, is in conflict with God, because it is self–centred and self–pleasing. When we became a Christian, we gained a new nature that is both God–pleasing and God centred. When Jesus died on the cross, it was for our old sinful nature as well as for our sins. Our baptism in water, symbolized our old inherent sinful nature as being buried with Jesus Christ (Romans 6:6) and our being raised to live a new life with a new nature (Romans 6:4).

This means that now that we are a Christian, and have a new nature, we are no longer separated from God because of our old nature. We have a new nature as Christians, and that makes a huge difference. God has taken care of our past and He no longer holds our sin against us, so we are now able to relate to God devotionally, personally, relationally and intimately. Previously we could not, as we were far away and unable to relate to God in any way with that old nature. But now, as Christians, we have a new spiritual nature to help us in our struggle

Section A. Adversary Awareness

against sin and our tendency to wilfully disobey the God who is now our King and master. God has placed His Spirit within us, and the more we allow the Holy Spirit to control us, the stronger our new nature becomes. Our old nature has gone and has been burned and buried. Though sometimes it will refuse to lie down. We are to continue living as if we are always wearing our new nature like a new coat, so that as His follower, we can be seen to be living a life worthy of His Holy name.

As Christians, followers of Jesus Christ, we are now God's ambassadors (2 Corinthians 5:20). We live within a constant battle, as our new inherited nature battles our old sinful nature. Sin is a constant thorn in our side. However, we are not to continue the "practice of sinning" (1 John 5:18). How are we to deal with sin? In order to deal with it, we find it helpful to understand first of all what sin is, then the cycle of sin and then finally, how we as Christians can deal with sins in our life.

How can sin be described? Sin is anything that separates humans from God, which consequently leads to both a spiritual and physical death. Sin is a lack of conformity to the Moral Law of God, either in deeds, attitudes, or inclination. Sin is a missing of the mark set by God, just as an arrow missing its intended target. All sin is sin in relation to God and this leads to an impaired relationship between the sinner and the Lord of All. Sin is never our friend, despite all its enticements and lures. Sin is an evasive intruder into our life, looking to steal our very life. Sin dehumanises us because it seeks to take away a portion of who we are in Christ. Jesus said the two greatest commands were to love God and to love other people (Matthew 22:36–40). Any breakage of those two commandments is therefore sin. That is, sin is a failing to meet God's standards of behaviour and life.

There are two kinds of sin. Firstly, there are the sins of commission, which are when we actively do things we should not do. These are where God's commands are actively broken. Then there are sins of omission, which are the passive kinds of sin where we are not doing as we ought, and we fail to do things we should do.

"If anyone, then, knows the good they ought to do and doesn't do it, it is sin for them." (James 4:17)

As Christians, through our old nature, we were enslaved to sin and powerless to free ourselves (John 8:34, Romans 6:19–20). The same is true for all humans, as all people are sinners against God (Romans 3:23; 1 Kings 8:46), with the notable exception of the Lord Jesus Christ (Hebrews 4:15). There is no conceivable position of neutrality. We were born sinful and we are therefore guilty before God. Guilty because God is a holy and righteous God, who cannot abide sin in any shape or form. Even as Christians and as one who has accepted Jesus as their Lord and Saviour, sin still has an effect upon us. Unsurprisingly.

However, unlike unbelievers who are separated from God due to sin, as Christians when we sin, we mar only the fellowship we enjoy with Jesus. Separation has not occurred because Jesus still has us firmly by the hand. Jesus has a strong grip upon us. That does not mean as Christians that we are to deliberately and wilfully sin. It is not necessary, advisable or sensible to do so. Sin in our life is never be tolerated but is to be dealt with.

The Apostle John commands that as Christians, we are not to continue the practise of sinning (1 John 3:6). Why? Because we are commanded to walk in the light of Jesus (1 John 1:7). We used to think that our eternal life would start when we died. The eternal life that we are promised, we are to start living right now. How? We are to live in the way that we shall live with Christ in the new heavens and the new earth (Revelation 21:1). Our eternal life has begun! But if we are honest, we have to admit that we do sometimes stray and commit sin. What are we to do about it? One man who knew what to do was King David. We read of his reactions to his sin, where he speaks of his confession of sin to God (Psalm 51) and His promised abandonment of it (Psalm 32). David's response to confessing his sin was like this:

Section A. Adversary Awareness

> [5] Then I acknowledged my sin to you
> and did not cover up my iniquity.
> I said, 'I will confess my transgressions to the LORD.'
> And you forgave the guilt of my sin.
> [6] Therefore let all the faithful pray to you
> while you may be found;
> surely the rising of the mighty waters will not reach them.
> [7] You are my hiding–place; you will protect me from trouble and surround me with songs of deliverance. (Psalm 32:5–7)

That is also to be our reaction when we sin. We are not to just ignore it. Neither are we to wallow in self–pity concerning our sinfulness. We are to take God's view of it and call it what it is. Sin. Nor are we to claim that we are without sin. Why? Because if we do that, then we are living in self–delusion and we are making God out to be a liar (1 John 1:10). When we realise that we have indeed sinned, we are to confess it quickly and ask for God's forgiveness. God is faithful and He will forgive us our sins, when we come to Him in penitence and faith. Why do we do this? Simply so that our relationship with Him is not marred, marked or disrupted.

> [8] If we claim to be without sin, we deceive ourselves and the truth is not in us. [9] If we confess our sins, He is faithful and just and will forgive us our sins and purify us from all unrighteousness. [10] If we claim we have not sinned, we make Him out to be a liar and His word is not in us. (1 John 1:8–10)

That is why at the end of each day, it is a good idea to include a simple prayer of general confession so that our fellowship with Jesus is not scarred. That is why in a lot of Churches, there is a general confession at the start of their worship services. Jesus wants us to have complete fellowship with Him, and by confessing our sin, our fellowship with Him is made all the richer.

> [40] Then He returned to His disciples and found them sleeping. 'Couldn't you men keep watch with me for one hour?' He asked Peter. [41] 'Watch and pray so that you will not fall into temptation. The spirit is willing, but the flesh is weak.'
> (Matthew 26:40–41)

> [12] So, if you think you are standing firm, be careful that you don't fall! [13] No temptation has overtaken you except what is common to mankind. And God is faithful; He will not let you be tempted beyond what you can bear. But when you are tempted, He will also provide a way out so that you can endure it.
> (1 Corinthians 10:12–13)

As we face temptation to sin, sometimes we do stumble, succumb to those temptations and sin against God. It's an undeniable and inevitable fact of the Christian disciple's life. But it is good to know that temptations are common experiences for all Christians , and not just for us as an individual. No matter what we may think at the time or what Satan tries to tell us.

An important thing for us to continue to note and remember, is that temptation in and of itself, is not sin. Rather it is the giving in to the temptation that constitutes sin. One of the keys to living a righteous life and not sinning is by dealing with temptations at the very moment they confront us. Part of dealing with temptation is to know the strategy of the devil as he tries to trap us. The Bible tells us that as Christians, we can expect to face temptation from three different angles: Satan, our old nature and the world.

In the Bible, the word 'world' does not always refer to the physical universe. It is often used to describe the community of sinful men and women that possesses a spirit of rebellion against God (1 John 5:19). Because of its opposition to God, the world values those things God hates (1 John 2:16). Its temptations to the believer are twofold: lust for

Section A. Adversary Awareness

the sensual and pride in life. Love of the world and its actions, morals and values, produces in our life these four things if we don't stop it and cut it off. It leads to a turning away from the Lord's work as well as from other Christians (2 Timothy 4:10). It leads to alienation from God (James 4:4), engaging in corrupting sins (2 Peter 1:4; 1 John 2:15–17) and being deceived by false teachers (1 John 4:1; 2 John 7). To overcome the love of the world, we need to love God with an even greater love (1 John 2:15).

'Flesh' in the Bible refers to the bad things that well up from deep inside us, as the sinful nature which is opposed to God (Romans 8:7). Some examples of these actions are given by Paul:

> [19] The acts of the flesh are obvious: sexual immorality, impurity and debauchery; [20] idolatry and witchcraft; hatred, discord, jealousy, fits of rage, selfish ambition, dissensions, factions [21] and envy; drunkenness, orgies, and the like. I warn you, as I did before, that those who live like this will not inherit the kingdom of God. (Galatians 5:19–21)

If our lives were to be characterized by these sins, then we could not be a true Christian and we would remain under the wrath of God (Ephesians 2:3). Though the flesh, this old nature which is sinful, is not destroyed for the Christian, we do not need to obey it (Romans 7:15–8:3). As Christians, we now possess a new nature empowered by the Holy Spirit who has come to live within us. Since the flesh and the Holy Spirit are totally opposed to each other, the one which the Christian believer allows to dominate, will take charge in their life and produce its own fruit: Fruit of the Spirit or fruit of the flesh.

The solution to the urges of the flesh lies in acknowledging and remembering that the power of sin was broken by Jesus' death on the cross (Romans 6:6, 11 & 14) and by living under the control of the Holy Spirit who lives within us as God's children (Galatians 5:16). It is a constant dependence in faith on the Holy Spirit's power. We must choose, by a definitive act of our will, to benefit from the Spirit's counsel, power and assistance.

Satan has an obvious role to play in temptations we face as Christians. With regard to our life as Christians, Satan will constantly endeavour to accuse us (Revelation 12:10), deceive us (2 Corinthians 11:14), devour our testimony for Jesus Christ (1 Peter 5:8) and hinder our work for God (1 Thessalonians 2:18). As we stand firmly together in the faith (1 Peter 5:9) and wear the full armour of God (Ephesians 6:10–17), Satan will flee.

One of the best ways for us to oppose these adversaries is for us to grow as Christians, being continually transformed under the guidance of the Holy Spirit and submit to Him all that we do and are. As Christians, our love for God must always be stronger than our love for the world. If we love somebody, we do not want to hurt that person. When we go against God and sin against Him, we are hurting our relationship with Him. He is a holy God and cannot abide any sin. As we grow and develop as Christians, our love of God grows and develops, and therefore our desire to sin grows less.

Temptation is common to all Christians. I know that it is certainly true from my daily experience of being a Christian now for 40 years. However, we also know that God always provides a way out so that we do not have to succumb to temptation (1 Corinthians 10:12–13). A great thing for us to remember, which we often forget, is that the Holy Spirit dwells in us, lives within us , and we are told from God's Word, that the One who is within us, is far superior and greater than the one who is in the world, the evil one (1 John 4:4). Now that is a comforting thought, is it not. Why? Because it means we don't face those temptations alone. As we are confronted with temptation, we can pray and ask for God's help to resist. It may also mean that we are to avoid the situation or circumstance where we are being tempted.

Another good thing we should have, is to have a couple of people to gracefully hold us accountable to our overcoming these temptations

Section A. Adversary Awareness

and to pray with and for us. That takes our being completely honest with them and them also being honest with us. This is, of course, contrary to the ways and actions of Satan, the father of lies and Prince of this world. Therefore, when we do sin, we are to repent of our sins. Repentance can be defined as feeling pain, or regret for something done or not done; a change of mind, or conduct, because of regret; or having sorrow or regret over an action or inaction. These definitions are of course true, at least in part.

But for the Christian, repentance means much more than these ideas. Repentance, for the Christian, is a voluntary change of mind, in which the Christian turns from a life of sin to living a life of righteousness. The Greek word translated as 'repent' has a basic meaning of 'turn around and go the other way'. "Repent!" would be shouted by the Roman officer to his soldiers. In other words, turn around now and go the other way quickly.

The importance of repentance was vital to the teaching of John the Baptist (Matthew 3:1–2), Jesus (Matthew 4:17; Mark 1:15) and the Apostles (Acts 2:38, 20:21). Additionally, we know that God commands repentance (Acts 17:30) and that it is God's will that all people repent (1 Timothy 2:4; 2 Peter 3:9).

This repentance is done in the three spheres of our life. Firstly, concerning the heart, or our emotions, which is revealed through genuine sorrow for our sin. This is a godly sorrow which leads us to repentance before God (2 Corinthians 7:8–10).Secondly, in reference to our mind, the intellect, where we recognize mentally our personal sinfulness and guilt before God (Psalm 51:3; Romans 3:20). Then lastly, through our will, which is disclosed through our decision to turn from all sin and a life which is self–pleasing and self–centred back to a righteous life wholly devoted to God alone and serving Him alone (Matthew 21:28–32).

When we became Christians, our sins were forgiven through Jesus' death on the Cross. That is when we had our 'bath' as it were. That is the point in our life when we were completely justified before Almighty God. That is when we were accepted by Him and declared to be His child. Having been justified already, we don't need a bath anymore. But we do need the equivalent of a foot washing daily. Every time we partake of the Holy Communion, we are to confess our sins before our God and turn away from them, having accepted His generous forgiveness. God through His wellsprings of grace and mercy forgives us, cleanses us and our intimate relationship with Him is unhindered, unfettered and unbroken. Amazing.

Section A. Adversary Awareness

Encouragement From Other Sojourners

The devil does not sleep, nor is the flesh yet dead; therefore, you must never cease your preparation for battle, because on the right and on the left are enemies who never rest.[6]

Original sin, then, may be defined as the hereditary corruption and depravity of our nature. This reaches every part of the soul, makes us abhorrent to God's wrath and produces in us what Scripture calls the works of the flesh. ... Sins are the fruits of sin.[7]

... a Christian is not a man who never goes wrong, but a man who is enabled to repent and pick Himself up and begin over again after each stumble – because the Christ–life is inside Him, repairing Him all the time, enabling Him to repeat (in some degree) the kind of voluntary death which Christ Himself carried out.[8]

Original sin, after regeneration, is like a word that begins to heal; though it is a wound, yet it is in course of healing, though it still runs and is sore.
So original sin remains in Christians until they die, yet itself is mortified and continually dying. Its head is crushed in pieces, so that it cannot condemn us.[9]

---

[6] à Kempis, Page 53
[7] Calvin, Page 90
[8] Lewis01, Page 63
[9] Luther, Page 154

A3. The World

[18] 'If the world hates you, keep in mind that it hated me first. [19] If you belonged to the world, it would love you as its own. As it is, you do not belong to the world, but I have chosen you out of the world. That is why the world hates you. [20] Remember what I told you: "A servant is not greater than His master." If they persecuted me, they will persecute you also. If they obeyed my teaching, they will obey yours also. [21] They will treat you this way because of my name, for they do not know the one who sent me. [22] If I had not come and spoken to them, they would not be guilty of sin; but now they have no excuse for their sin. [23] Whoever hates me hates my Father as well. [24] If I had not done among them the works no one else did, they would not be guilty of sin. As it is, they have seen, and yet they have hated both me and my Father. [25] But this is to fulfil what is written in their Law: "They hated me without reason." [26] 'When the Advocate comes, whom I will send to you from the Father – the Spirit of truth who goes out from the Father – He will testify about me. [27] And you also must testify, for you have been with me from the beginning. (John 15:18–27)

Satan has control over this world at the current time. It is his kingdom and domain. Likewise, with regards to our second adversary, every person in this world, was born with an old nature which was inherently sinful and anti–God. Satan has dominion over this world and we have to deal with people who are still under control of their old nature, because they don't have this new nature that Christians have. How is the world engaged in part of our spiritual battle, as Christians? There are two main areas where Satan demonstrates his control over this world and where the old nature of people flourishes. That is in regard to government we live under and the culture we live within.

Section A. Adversary Awareness

GOVERNMENT

Firstly, we look together at government. All people all over the world live under a form of leadership or government. That government may be democratically elected, a monarchy or even an oppressive dictatorship. Whatever kind of government we find ourselves under, we have one. If there was not a government in place, as hard as it is to imagine, total chaos would reign, and people would just do whatever pleases them, regardless of consequences and regardless of other people. What does the Bible say should be our reaction and attitude to the government. By government, we mean all levels of government and authority, from local to federal or national government.

> [1] Let everyone be subject to the governing authorities, for there is no authority except that which God has established. The authorities that exist have been established by God. [2] Consequently, whoever rebels against the authority is rebelling against what God has instituted, and those who do so will bring judgment on themselves. [3] For rulers hold no terror for those who do right, but for those who do wrong. Do you want to be free from fear of the one in authority? Then do what is right and you will be commended. [4] For the one in authority is God's servant for your good. But if you do wrong, be afraid, for rulers do not bear the sword for no reason. They are God's servants, agents of wrath to bring punishment on the wrongdoer. [5] Therefore, it is necessary to submit to the authorities, not only because of possible punishment but also as a matter of conscience.
>
> [6] This is also why you pay taxes, for the authorities are God's servants, who give their full time to governing. [7] Give to everyone what you owe them: if you owe taxes, pay taxes; if revenue, then revenue; if respect, then respect; if honour, then honour. (Romans 13:1–7)

Engaged in Battle

What is the function of human government? Paul indicates that there are at least three functions of a human government. Human government, as thought by Paul, was to promote the broad–spectrum welfare of all the community and not just select groups, where its laws are in effect. With all this in mind, how is Christians to respond to the government we find ourselves under?

From the moment Adam sinned, it was plainly obvious that human civilizations would need some form of restraint and law, in order to protect their citizens. This is clearly seen in the incident, where Roman soldiers step in to save Paul from being killed by other people in Jerusalem (Acts 21). Paul stipulates that duly appointed government officials and servants are to be considered as servants of God (even if they don't believe in God.).

In response to these, how then, should we as Christians respond to government and governments? The Apostle Peter helps us here:

> [13] Submit yourselves for the Lord's sake to every human authority: whether to the emperor, as the supreme authority, [14] or to governors, who are sent by Him to punish those who do wrong and to commend those who do right.
>
> [15] For it is God's will that by doing good you should silence the ignorant talk of foolish people. [16] Live as free people, but do not use your freedom as a cover–up for evil; live as God's slaves. [17] Show proper respect to everyone, love the family of believers, fear God, honour the emperor. (1 Peter 2:13–17)

Strong words there from Peter. Paul offers further words of wisdom.

> [1] I urge, then, first of all, that petitions, prayers, intercession and thanksgiving be made for all people – [2] for kings and all those in authority, that we may live peaceful and quiet lives in all godliness and holiness. [3] This is good, and pleases God our Saviour, [4] who wants all people to be saved and to come to a knowledge of the truth. (1 Timothy 2:1–3)

Section A. Adversary Awareness

From these passages of Scripture, it is clearly impossible to be simultaneously a solid Christian and a poor citizen. A government professes responsibilities towards us as one of its citizens, and we also as Christians, have responsibilities towards our government, regardless of the type of government we live under.

Firstly, we have a responsibility to recognize and acknowledge that God ordains the government. We see that from the writing of Paul during the time when the Emperor Nero was in power and systematically persecuting and torturing Christians (Romans 13). There is no authority given to humanity except as permitted by God. Even to the most sadistic, dictatorial or atheist governments – they have power only because God has allowed them. So we are to obey our government. However, this is not to be a slavish obedience regardless of what laws are decreed. By no means, no. The exception to this is where obedience to the government would require us as Christians to either actively or passively, disobey God and fall into sin. For as Christians believer, we are to live in complete obedience to God rather than any government or human (Acts 4:18–20).

Secondly, as much as we probably hate to, we are commanded to pay taxes to the government. For by doing so, the government should set about ensuring, for example, that the weaker and more vulnerable sections of the community are cared for, helped and protected.

Thirdly, and quite possibly, most importantly, we are to pray for our leaders, governments and those in authority. To pray for them is to show love towards them and it is also a way for God to shine into the lives of people. One of the things we are to pray for, is that the government governs righteously, honourably, honestly and with integrity. As Christians, as citizens, we are free to be law–abiding, conscious that we are under submission to Almighty God. It also means giving respect to all members of society from the lowest to the highest. As Christians, we are to submit ourselves to our government and be living lives worthy of the Gospel of Christ. This may indeed win some for God, win the recognition of their government as well as influencing government conduct, policy and law. Whatever government we find ourselves under, we are to pray for our leaders even if we thoroughly disagree with some or all of their actions. They are in power, only because God has allowed them. They will answer to Him one day for what they have done with the power given to them by God alone. God is in ultimate control, and He is on the ultimate throne and is the definitive power.

Culture

To our second word where Satan and the old nature exhibit control over the world. Culture. Cultures from around this world are individual, unique and diverse. There are thousands of different cultures to be found in the nations around the world. From these many different cultures, there are many differences which are rich in variety and stark in contrast. Within each of them, things can be found that we like or dislike and discover differences and similarities to the culture that we were raised in and the culture in which we live.

Some of what we are as a person, is because of the culture we were born into and raised within. The things that are acceptable to us in a cultural sense, may well shock you, because of your cultural upbringing. Take for example, an El Salvadorian wedding I attended back in the 1980's. The husband at the post–service reception places his wife's left leg on a chair, discreetly lift her dress to the upper thigh and proceeds to pull her garter off with his teeth! This is in front of everybody! He then throws the garter to a gathered group of single men, all eagerly waiting to catch it! Now if you are offended by this, it is probably because of your upbringing in a culture, where at a wedding, this is not the best behaviour. Just because something is different from our own culture, does not necessarily mean that it is wrong. Our cultural heritage and upbringing affects our ethics,

Section A. Adversary Awareness

lifestyle, family values, and worldview. Culture also has a place and a say in regard to our Christianity. Some cultures insist that a person follows a particular religion out of respect for tradition, whether that is Hinduism, Buddhism, Islam, Zionism, Taoism, Shintoism, Spiritism or any other 'ism' which is that cultural norm. Christianity is tolerated as long as it doesn't impinge and impact on other religions or customs. Sometimes there are severe pressures and penalties to pay if a person wanted to change their religion, say to Christianity from Islam.

As Christians, followers of Jesus Christ, we hold firm assuredly that Jesus Christ, was God, is God and always will be God. Therefore, what does Jesus have to say about culture and cultural differences? We know that Jesus kept all the cultural traditions, as a good Jewish man, and this neither affected His own personal holiness or offended those to whom He engaged in a cross–cultural exchange. Whether it was with a Roman centurion; a Canaanite woman; Samaritans; Greeks or other cultures, Jesus was always sensitive to their particular problems regardless of His own cultural traditions, which included not touching or talking to foreigners, women, sick and poor people. He continually broke the traditional cultural religious taboos, by doing these things, and that is one of the reasons that Jewish authorities hated Him and plotted to kill Him.

Some people may think that we are Christians because we were raised in a Christian country and it was our cultural tradition to follow this Jesus. Some may also think that Jesus is only for the Jewish people and those in the West where Christianity is seen as the "normal" religion. Others may also be thinking that Christianity is not for them because their tradition and culture say that they must follow another religion and not change.

As part of my own testimony, I am a Christian because Jesus was pursuing me! It is true, that my upbringing in a country which at least is nominally Christian did pay a small part in my turning to follow Jesus Christ. But by becoming a Christian, I rebelled against my parents and against my Australian culture. The main reason however, that any of us are a Christian, is because Jesus Christ was chasing each of us. We made a conscious decision to follow Him. Jesus is and always will be the Son of God, the saviour for all people of all nations, languages and cultures for all time. Jesus said that He will draw all people to Himself (John 12:32).

To be holy, following Jesus Christ as Lord, and growing in righteousness can be hard for us. Why? Because the Christian life is demanding and yet also exciting! We use all sorts of excuses for sinning. We may sometimes use the excuse that is part of our individual cultural identity to do that, so it can't be wrong! In some cultures, a man can have more than one wife; in still other cultures men treat women as a little lower than slaves or dogs. Some cultures are well known for its arrogance, insulting and being rude to all and sundry. Other cultures place emphasis on gross materialism & collecting possessions at all costs. Yet other cultures allow indifference to the suffering of the poor and sick in their community, putting their low position in society down to bad luck, kismet or fate.

Now we know that all these things are wrong because the Bible clearly states they are wrong. The Bible says only have one partner in marriage, love and respect each other (1 Corinthians 7:1–5). The Bible says love one another (John 13:34–35); forgive each other (Ephesians 4:32) don't be rude but be humble and not arrogant(Philippians 2:3). When our cultural traditions cross over the lines of sin, drawn out for us in the Bible, then we must at all costs to ourselves, stop doing them. We don't have to do away with all our cultural traditions, just those that are clearly unbiblical and hinder our path to following Jesus closely. Jesus has the victory. In some final teaching before He goes to the cross, He has these words to say about Satan's dominion, the world:

> [33] "I have told you these things, so that in me you may have peace. In this world you will have trouble. But take heart! I have overcome the world." (John 16:33)

Section A. Adversary Awareness

Encouragement From Other Sojourners

He who follows Me, walks not in darkness," says the Lord (John 8:12). By these words of Christ we are advised to imitate His life and habits, if we wish to be truly enlightened and free from all blindness of heart. Let our chief effort, therefore, be to study the life of Jesus Christ.[10]

But there is another meaning *'of the world'* in the New Testament. Sometimes the world is seen as an organized system of human civilisation and activity which is opposed to God and alienated from him. It represents everything that prevents man from loving, and therefore obeying, his creator.[11]

Enemy–occupied territory – that is what this world is. Christianity is the story of how the rightful king has landed, you might say landed in disguise, and is calling us to take part in a great campaign of sabotage.[12]

The world will neither hold God for God, nor the devil for the devil. And if a man were left to himself, to do after his own kind and nature, he would willingly throw our Lord God out at the window; for the world regards God nothing at all, as the Psalm says: The wicked man saith in his heart, there is no God.[13]

---

[10] à Kempis. Page 5
[11] Jackman, Page 60
[12] Lewis01, Page 46
[13] Luther, Page 82

Engaged in Battle

Section B: The Armour We Wear

If the devil, sin, our old nature and the world are our adversaries, enemies and foes, what can we as Christians do about it?

> [10] Finally, be strong in the Lord and in His mighty power. [11] Put on the full armour of God, so that you can take your stand against the devil's schemes. [12] For our struggle is not against flesh and blood, but against the rulers, against the authorities, against the powers of this dark world and against the spiritual forces of evil in the heavenly realms.
> [13] Therefore put on the full armour of God, so that when the day of evil comes, you may be able to stand your ground, and after you have done everything, to stand. [14] Stand firm then, with the belt of truth buckled round your waist, with the breastplate of righteousness in place, [15] and with your feet fitted with the readiness that comes from the gospel of peace.
> [16] In addition to all this, take up the shield of faith, with which you can extinguish all the flaming arrows of the evil one. [17] Take the helmet of salvation and the sword of the Spirit, which is the word of God. (Ephesians 6:10–17)

Section B. The Armour We Wear

As Christians, those who are following Jesus Christ, there is often great pressure from our adversaries to compromise our life of faith, whereby we are intimidated to be disobedient to God. We get those insatiable thoughts of lust, revenge or pride. Doubts set in. Guilt appears constant. To help us endure, God has designed spiritual armour to be worn during this battle. This armour is what God wears when He goes out to battle, according to Isaiah.

> [15] Truth is nowhere to be found,
> and whoever shuns evil becomes a prey.
> The LORD looked and was displeased
> that there was no justice.
> [16] He saw that there was no one,
> he was appalled that there was no one to intervene;
> so His own arm achieved salvation for Him,
> and His own righteousness sustained Him.
> [17] He put on righteousness as His breastplate,
> and the helmet of salvation on His head;
> he put on the garments of vengeance
> and wrapped Himself in zeal as in a cloak.
> (Isaiah 59:15–17)

One final thought to bear in mind before we proceed further, is that Paul's instructions were to the Church in Ephesus, a group of people. So the armour is not just for a Christian to put on as an individual, but also as part of a local Church or group of Christians together. All the while, encouraging each other to do so as individuals.

Encouragement From Other Sojourners

"Be strong," says he, "in the Lord, and in the strength of His might." That is, in the hope which we have in Him, by means of His aid. For as he had enjoined many duties, which were necessary to be done, fear not, he seems to say, cast your hope upon the Lord, and He will make all easy.[14]

The Christian's armour is made to be worn – no taking it off until you have finished your course. Your armour and your garment of flesh come off together. … In heaven you shall appear, not in armour, but in robes of glory. Nevertheless, for the present you must wear your assigned suit night and day. You must walk, work, and sleep in it or you are not a true soldier of Christ.[15]

We are to take unto us the whole armour of God, and also we are to put it on. Then we shall be able to withstand, and to stand. The conflict here is mainly viewed as being defensive. We are set in an exalted and heavenly position by the grace of our God, and there we stand in spite of every attempt to dislodge us.[16]

There is no protection, there is nothing we can do, that will ultimately protect us against this wily subtle, powerful enemy but the armour of God Himself. Essentially, of course, it is the armour that is provided by God.[17]

---

[14] Chrysostom, Page 295
[15] Gurnall01, Page 76
[16] Hole, Page 62–63
[17] Lloyd-Jones01, Page 175–176

Section B. The Armour We Wear

God Himself has provided us with a complete protection, so that nothing the devil throws at us might bring us down. All we have to do is put the armour on. We need not fear the enemy. … We are, rather, to square up to the adversary, to get our courage from God, to join battle, and to trust that God's almighty power will cause us to prevail. [18]

Wobbly Christians have no firm foothold in Christ are an easy prey of the devil. And Christians who shake like reeds and rushes cannot resist the wind when the principalities and powers being to blow. Paul wants to see Christians so strong and stable that they remain firm even against the devil's wiles and even in the evil day, that is, in a time of special pressure. For such stability, both of character and in crisis, the armour of God is essential.[19]

God gives us all the protection we need. We must see that there is a 'ring of truth' about our walk with the Lord, that our lives are right ('righteous') with God and with one another, that we seek to make peace wherever we go, that w lift up that shield of faith together to quench all the flaming darts of the evil one, that we protect our minds from fears and anxieties that easily assail, and that we use God's word to good effect in the power of the Spirit.[20]

---

[18] Olyott, Page 135–136
[19] Stott, Page 275
[20] Watson, Page 183

B1. Belt of Truth

> [1] Dear friends, do not believe every spirit, but test the spirits to see whether they are from God, because many false prophets have gone out into the world. [2] This is how you can recognise the Spirit of God: every spirit that acknowledges that Jesus Christ has come in the flesh is from God, [3] but every spirit that does not acknowledge Jesus is not from God. This is the spirit of the antichrist, which you have heard is coming and even now is already in the world. (1 John 4:1–3)

Truth is the belt which holds all other items of the armour in place. Today we hear constantly that there are no absolute truths anymore. People and society say "What is true for us may not be true for you. What is true for you may not be true for me."

What, therefore, is truth? The idea of truth in the Old Testament was used in two ways. Firstly, facts may be either true or false – an intellectual truth. An example would be that Moses existed as a person. That is a fact. It is therefore self–evidently true.

Truth can also be used to define a characteristic of a reliable person, such as the test of Joseph's brothers (Genesis 42:16). These truths are also used to describe God as a true God, rather than the pagan gods belonging to the nations around Israel. Truth, or being true, is described as a characteristic of Yahweh, the God of Israel. He is consistently true and therefore is undeniably trustworthy in all His ways. God's loving care is trustworthy and is seen throughout His dealings with Israel.

In the New Testament, Christianity itself is seen as truth (Galatians 2:5; Ephesians 1:13). Indeed, Jesus, the head of the Church, said that He was the only truth, the only life and the only way to God (John 14:6). Furthermore, truth is God's word to be obeyed actively and not dismissed passively. What role is active truth to play in our life as Christians? Having and possessing a growing knowledge of biblical

Section B. The Armour We Wear

truth enables our character to develop, building our spiritual strength and maturity. Since understanding the Bible increases our knowledge of God, it also increases the possibilities for us to reveal to others, our transformation by Jesus. A transformation where we are seen to love, grow and serve.

Ignorance leads to mere superstition and not a life of devotion to God. God's truth combats error. Satan uses his disdainful distortion of the Bible to put people off the truth. Therefore, we need to get to know what the Bible states, so that we will not be led into error by Satan and those people who would want to deceive us (1 John 4:1–3).

However, for truth to be effective, it needs to be a truth with life in it. That is where we will be an active doer of the Bible's suggestions and commands and not merely a passive hearer. Our life as Christians is to be a balance of love and truth. They must coexist with each other in our thinking. Then through that knowledge, service and faith in Almighty God, we will continually grow and be strengthened in all aspects of our life. All to His praise, glory and honour alone. As we wear the belt of truth, we will be growing more like Jesus Christ in every aspect of our daily life.

> "But the fruit of the Spirit is love, joy, peace, patience, kindness, goodness, faithfulness, gentleness and self–control. Against such things there is no law. Those who belong to Christ Jesus have crucified the sinful nature with its passions and desires. Since we live by the Spirit, let us keep in step with the Spirit." (Galatians 5:22–25)

Growing more like Jesus is a lifelong process. In the words of the Bible, it is one of the big words – sanctification. 'Sanctify' is one of the words used in English to translate a connected set of Hebrew or Greek words. Other words include holy, saintly, and consecrate. A rather mixed lot. Looking at them all together gives a good idea what they all mean. They are all to do with the long and difficult process by which an ordinary person, like us, gets to be more like Jesus Christ. If we, as disciples of Jesus Christ, are showing the fruit of the Spirit, then we are becoming Christ–like and we are being sanctified. Sometimes that growth as Christians is a difficult path for us, but nobody said that it would be easy. Certainly, Jesus never said that it would be. Another way to look at growing or sanctification, is that it is like the changing of a caterpillar into a butterfly – it's a process. As we grow more like Jesus Christ, this gives people a reason to ask why we seem to be so different. This process of sanctification affects every aspect of our life as we mature in Jesus Christ, for we are being transformed and becoming more like Him.

> "And we know that in all things God works for the good of those who love Him, who have been called according to His purpose. For those God foreknew He also predestined to be conformed to the likeness of His Son, that He might be the firstborn among many brothers and sisters."
> (Romans 8:28–29)

> 'And we all, who with unveiled faces contemplate the Lord's glory, are being transformed into His image with ever–increasing glory, which comes from the Lord, who is the Spirit.'
> (2 Corinthians 3:18)

When we became Christians, we started an exciting journey in the Christian life. Living Christians life which is pleasing to God, is not an accident, but is a direct result of living in harmony with the basic principles of life set forth in the Bible. We are aware that the Christian life is not a matter of expecting spiritual maturity to occur overnight.

> [16] All Scripture is God–breathed and is useful for teaching, rebuking, correcting and training in righteousness, [17] so that the servant of God may be thoroughly equipped for every good work. (2 Timothy 3:16–17)

Section B. The Armour We Wear

The Bible lays down standards and principles of living. Through reading and studying the Bible, we learn what God expects of us and what guidelines He has given us to achieve this quality of life. As we apply the principles and guidelines of the Bible to our life, we are continually transformed into the likeness of Christ – which is the journey we are on. A happy and good life is possible. Jesus, the Lord and Master of all Christians, said:

"I have come that they may have life, and have it to the full."
(John 10:10)

This is achieved as we allow Jesus Christ to live this life through us so that we start to think and respond like He would do, to the people and circumstances around us. We continue to learn how to see circumstances and people from God's perspective, rather than reacting on the basis of our own feelings and perspective. When we respond to circumstances on the basis of our feelings that is when conflict, stress, tension and depression confront us. When we respond to people and circumstances by looking from God's perspective, we build and reveal a transformed character. We become spiritually mature and live a life which is being transformed into the image of Jesus Christ and worthy of His name. This is done by remembering to do it in the power of the Holy Spirit living within us. Living in our own strength may get some limited success, but if we rely on the power of the Holy Spirit, we will live a whole life that is worthy of Jesus Christ.

We wear the belt of truth.

Encouragement From Other Sojourners

If we fortify ourselves with this, if we "gird ourselves with truth," then shall no one overcome us. ... He, however, who "is girt about with the truth," first, never is weary; and secondly, if he should be weary, he will rest himself upon the truth itself.[21]

Truth lives to reign in peace with those who are now willing to suffer for it. Christian, do you not want to be one of those victors who shall ride beside Christ's triumphant chariot into the heavenly city and take a crown with the faithful saints who stood in the militant days when Christ and His truth battled Satan here on earth? With your thoughts, wipe away the tears and blood which now cover the face of suffering truth and present it to your eyes as it will look in glory.[22]

All our activities are to be circumscribed by truth. The truth is to govern us. The truth is given to us by God, but we are to put it on, so that it may govern us. God's word is truth; but it is not truth in the Bible which is going to defend us, but rather truth applied in a practical way to all our activities.[23]

Truth does matter! If you begin to go wrong in your 'communications', in what you say to one another and in your thoughts, it will lead to bad practice, bad manners, and bad behaviour. And eventually you will make shipwreck of the faith.[24]

---

[21] Chrysostom, Page 303–304
[22] Gurnall02, Page 45
[23] Hole, Page 63
[24] Lloyd-Jones01, Page 192

Section B. The Armour We Wear

The first thing a soldier donned was his protective apron, or girdle. It was like a thick leather belt ... In the same way the Christian believer is to bind himself round with 'truth'. It is the first thing he must be sure of before he goes to battle.[25]

Usually made of leather, the soldier's belt belonged rather to his underwear than his armour. Yet it was essential. It gathered his tunic together and also held his sword. It ensure that he was unimpeded when marching. As he buckled it on, it gave him a sense of hidden strength and confidence.[26]

---

[25] Olyott, Page 136
[26] Stott, Page 277

B2. Breastplate of Righteousness

> [21] But now apart from the law the righteousness of God has been made known, to which the Law and the Prophets testify. [22] This righteousness is given through faith in[j] Jesus Christ to all who believe. There is no difference between Jew and Gentile, [23] for all have sinned and fall short of the glory of God, [24] and all are justified freely by His grace through the redemption that came by Christ Jesus. [25] God presented Christ as a sacrifice of atonement, through the shedding of His blood—to be received by faith. He did this to demonstrate His righteousness, because in His forbearance He had left the sins committed beforehand unpunished— [26] He did it to demonstrate His righteousness at the present time, so as to be just and the one who justifies those who have faith in Jesus. (Romans 3:21–26)

As Christians, we have a new identity and because of this, we are to stay faithful to Jesus and His will for us, regardless of all opposition and alternatives. What is more, there is help at hand for us to grasp, because the Holy Spirit lives within us as Comforter and Counsellor. By allowing Him to do this, we are standing alone and being faithful to Him. That is showing the righteousness of Jesus which has been bestowed upon us, because we are born again and Christians.

Satan brings pressure to bear on us as Christians to reduce our standards and our commitment to Jesus Christ. We undergo challenges from Satan and from those that don't like or understand us and who are constantly tempting us to do wrong things or not to do right things. Consequently, we are to be separate from sin but not separated from the sinful society where we live, work and recreate.

This is what Jesus meant when He said these words:

> [14] I have given them your word and the world has hated them, for they are not of the world any more than I am of the world. [15]

Section B. The Armour We Wear

> My prayer is not that you take them out of the world but that you protect them from the evil one. [16] They are not of the world, even as I am not of it. [17] Sanctify them by the truth; your word is truth. [18] As you sent me into the world, I have sent them into the world. [19] For them I sanctify myself, that they too may be truly sanctified. (John 17:14–19)

The key to this standing alone is that we are to have a constant identification with Jesus Christ in every aspect of our life including our thought life, attitudes, actions and in the words that we speak. However, as we live out our Christian life, we know that there are hindrances to identifying with Jesus.

Here are just three major areas that as Christians, we have to struggle through. Firstly, there is the fear of losing friends. To have the right friends of course, a person must be willing to have enemies. Jesus made friends on the basis of who would accept Him and His message. We may indeed be excluded from the company of those who reject Jesus (Luke 6:26).

Secondly, there is the insatiable desire to be like those who are not Christians. David envied the success of the godless, until he realized that his destiny was disaster if he didn't change his mind (Psalm 73). When David knew that he had God, he also discovered that he needed nothing or another person to have the fulfilment only God provides. Then finally, there is an inborn fear of our worrying what other people will think. This is a fear of being different and being scornfully laughed at. Therefore, if those are some of the hindrances, what are some of the keys in our overcoming these hindrances? We are to remember God's way of life is superior and leads to a fulfilled life, according to Jesus:

> [10] The thief comes only to steal and kill and destroy; I have come that they may have life and have it to the full. [11] 'I am the good shepherd. The good shepherd lays down His life for the sheep. (John 10:10–11)

As we Christians act as light and salt in the world, with the help of the Holy Spirit within us and empowering us, we will be co–operating with God and He will be being honoured and glorified (1 Peter 4:12–14). If we give people no reason to ask about the hope and faith that we have in Jesus, they probably won't ask us.

As Christians, we shouldn't apologize for what we know and believe to be a superior way of life. We should never apologise for engaging in the work of evangelism. However, that does not mean we should be arrogant about it because we are also commanded to walk with humility. We are to just be natural about it. We are to let our spiritual life be natural and our natural life be spiritual. One way to do this, is for us to hold onto the idea that we are not our own boss. We are to let Jesus take both the strain and glory. Those who reject us, are ultimately also rejecting Jesus.

How can we make the right decisions in questionable areas? When we are in a difficult situation and we have to make a correct decision in a questionable area, we can ask ourselves questions such as: "Does it bring glory to God (1 Corinthians 10:31)?" "Can we thank God for this activity?" Indeed, we ask ourselves, "Could Jesus accompany us in it and does what is being proposed, help to build a transformed Christian character (1 Corinthians 10:23–24)?" "Will this cause another Christian to sin/stumble (1 Corinthians 8:9–13)?"

We know beyond doubt, and have assurance that we can rely on the Holy Spirit to help us, asking for His help and guidance. If in doubt, we can forget the question or simply wait until the right time (Romans 14:22–23). We can also ask other Christians, for advice. Overall, we are to abstain from all appearances of evil (1 Thessalonians 5:22). Then as we do this, our worldview is being constantly changed and transformed. A worldview is the way we see the world in which we live, particularly what we think of how other people think and why they act the way they do. The part we are interested in, is that part of how we think about God and our relationship to Him.

Section B. The Armour We Wear

The prevalent view, particularly in the West, is exhibited by following what is commonly called the "Golden Rule ", which is "to do to others, what you would have them do to you." Furthermore, they say that there are no certainties or absolutes in life, simply your own individual perspective. This view says that 'morality is a private thing and what is right for you, may not be right for us and don't you dare tell us that we are wrong in any aspect of our life, because our morals are mine and mine alone, and that is our right.'

As for religion, this prevalent worldview suggests that all religions inevitably lead to some form of god or gods – that is if any god exists at all. This is seen in the prevalent view particularly in the West, which is that of Darwinism and Scientific Humanism. Humanists and atheists argue that human beings are merely a miniscule section in nature's rich spectrum, and that Darwinism explains not only how humans got here but that the purpose of humanity has evolved unrestrained biologically and sexually. This worldview sees no reason for a creator or any form of intelligent designer, as humanity merely evolved by pure chance and random variations.

Further to this, humanity is seen as nothing more than just one little twig, or cell, amongst the order of primates. All the while, admitting that humankind has probably evolved as far as they can and that there is no definitely accepted account of how life first began. This atheistic and naturalistic theory goes on to deny the very existence of a spiritual world and claims that emotions such as love, fear, hatred and guilt, and thoughts and feelings, are merely physical or chemical in origin.

Contrast these with Christians worldview. Humanistic views are entirely theoretical and are based entirely upon a basic presupposition that there cannot be any form of deity, whether personal or impersonal, and belief that any kind of faith is blind, non–evidential and irrational. Contrast those worldviews with Christians worldview which states that humanity, both male and female, is made in the image of God and reflects God.

"May God Himself, the God of peace, sanctify you through and through. May your whole spirit, soul and body be kept blameless at the coming of my Lord Jesus Christ. The one who calls you is faithful, and He will do it" (1 Thessalonians 5:23)

When God created humanity, it was in His own image that all humans were created. As Christians, we believe therefore, that the whole person, regardless of who they are or what they have done or will do, is valuable to God, and not just the spirit (1 Thessalonians 5:23). God created humanity, in His own image therefore higher than the animal world. Humanity subsequently rebelled and disobeyed God. God then took the initiative and promised a way out through His chosen Messiah. This Messiah was Jesus Christ, and He simultaneously had both divine and human natures. It was He, who as God, stepped into history and became confined for a short while by time and space. He was born so that when He died on the cross, it was to pay the price so that all of humanity could be freed from slavery to sin and disobedience, if only they chose to accept and believe in Him as God. He rose again physically from the dead, ascended into heaven and now sits at the right hand of the Father. Those who don't accept Him as Lord and Saviour will spend eternity apart from Him. Jesus Christ is the only way to God, and all other paths lead to ultimate destruction, despite the whispers and lies of Satan.

That is why Christianity is the only true and permanent hope for the world. As Christians, living in the 21st century, we are to place God first, others second and our own self last. That is the path that we as Christians are to walk, as we follow God alone and serving both Him and other people. As we do this, the worldview we maintain, sees that we will continue being transformed into the very image of Jesus Christ (Philippians 3:20–21).

We put on the breastplate of righteousness.

Section B. The Armour We Wear

Encouragement From Other Sojourners

As the breastplate is impenetrable, so also is righteousness, and by righteousness here he means a life of universal virtue. Such a life no one shall ever be able to overthrow; it is true, many wound him, but no one cuts through him, no, not the devil himself.[27]

A spiritual dagger – sin which hunts for the 'precious life' – is the lethal weapon Satan uses to stab the conscience (Proverbs 6:26). ... Righteousness and holiness are God's protection to defend the believer's conscience from all wounds inflicted by sin.[28]

We are the very righteousness of God in Christ, but it is when we as a consequence walk in practical righteousness that it acts as a breastplate, covering all our vital parts from the blows directed by our powerful foes.[29]

The breastplate of righteousness helps us in the first place by giving us a general sense of confidence, and this is essential in our warfare. If you enter into this fight with the devil uncertainly or hesitantly you are already defeated. We need confidence.[30]

---

[27] Chrysostom, Page 309
[28] Gurnall02, Page 149
[29] Hole, Page 63
[30] Lloyd-Jones01, Page 231

B3. Gospel Feet

¹ And so it was with me, brothers and sisters. When I came to you, I did not come with eloquence or human wisdom as I proclaimed to you the testimony about God. ² For I resolved to know nothing while I was with you except Jesus Christ and Him crucified. ³ I came to you in weakness with great fear and trembling. ⁴ My message and my preaching were not with wise and persuasive words, but with a demonstration of the Spirit's power, ⁵ so that your faith might not rest on human wisdom, but on God's power. (1 Corinthians 2:1–5)

The Gospel declares that "Jesus is Lord" (Romans 10:9). This was dangerous talk in New Testament times, as it was a direct challenge to the Roman Empire who taught "Caesar is Lord". The Gospel is Trinitarian, in that it is the Father's mysterious revelation through the Son's work on the cross in the power of the Spirit. The Gospel is also Three Dimensional in that it covers the breadth of the Bible – all of Scripture is about God's plan of Salvation; the depth of the cross of Jesus Christ and the length of God's mission.

The Gospel was, and is, anathema and unpopular to those outside of the Kingdom of God. In the New Testament, it was a direct challenge to the ancient Roman Empire. Today, this thinking is also here, particularly in those countries where Christianity is actively persecuted. The Gospel is never popular, and if it is, then it is not a truly Biblical Gospel. For instance, some Churches proclaim a false Gospel where financial and health prosperity is the central claim. This is a false Gospel where Jesus is a cure–all being the central claim. There is also a false Gospel wherever it is used for political purposes. The true Gospel of the New Testament is "Jesus and Him crucified" (1 Corinthians 2:2).

The claim that "Jesus is Lord of all" was a direct and dangerous challenge to the prevailing idea throughout the Roman empire that

Section B. The Armour We Wear

Caesar was Lord of all. Jesus' exclusive claim to be the only way, the only truth and the only life challenges pluralism and universalism. In the ancient world, as today, there are plenty of gods available, why would people settle for just the One true God. Particularly one who had died. A life of holiness, morality and right living challenges immorality. God's power challenges cultured intellect who consider it as mere babbling. Humility challenges pride, for to kneel at the cross, takes great humility and this would have been derided and classed as utter blathering nonsense. Where people are proud and cultured, the very thought of humbly kneeling before a God is anathema.

We can be shouted down if we dare exclaim that Jesus is Lord and the only acceptable path to God. We are told in the media and by people, that Jesus Christ is not significant, there are no such thing as moral absolutes anymore, that what's morally right for us, may not be right for others and we are stay out of others private business. Sex and sexuality are worshipped and adored as if they were gods in themselves. We live in an age of humanism, scientific materialism and hyper–rationalism, where people cynically laugh at Christians and say that we worship a dead man, if He even existed at all, and that we are fools for believing in a God.

Humility is not looked upon as a strength today. It is frowned upon as a weakness. The prevalent worldview in the western communities, says that if we want to get ahead in life, we need to be strong, show some backbone, don't ever back down to anybody or anything and most certainly, never admit that we were wrong and have made mistakes. The way of the Gospel, the way for the Christian, however, is for us to kneel before the Cross of Jesus Christ, admit our mistakes and sins and be prepared to serve and take up our own cross. This is directly antagonistic to the prevailing worldview and culture of the western community. They are quite willing to accept a harmless baby at Christmas, but not the violence of the cross that followed at Easter. Evangelism can only be truly effective when undertaken under an umbrella of prayer and the work of the Holy Spirit. It is the Holy Spirit's power and authority, which allows the skills and talents of all people, to be used as effective Gospel messengers. As Christians, we need to continually remind ourselves that it is Jesus Christ who is building the Church, and that with the Holy Spirit's power, we are neither alone nor powerless.

After all, He is the Holy Spirit of evangelism. That is why we need not fear the supposed rise of fundamental atheism, humanism, or any other religion or – "ism". We have the power of the living God within us, to equip and use us for His glory, honour and mission. People may be able to remove the supposed 'spirit of Christmas' from schools and other government buildings, but they can never take away the Spirit of Christ that indwells us and all Christians.

The world around us, with the help of Satan, likes to play clever tricks on us. But we are to be different, to be discerning and wise, as Jesus commanded, "be as shrewd as snakes and as innocent as doves." (Matthew 10:16)

We are to stay faithful to Jesus and that sometimes is difficult. It means staying faithful to Jesus and His will, regardless of any opposition and attractive alternatives which confront us. By doing this we will endure and remain faithful to Him. In doing so we will be strengthened and energized for the work that Jesus Christ, our God, has set for us to do, as part of His Church, His body, here in the world, wherever we go and whatever we are doing.

The early Church preached that God, who is outside of both time and space, entered human time and history as a human baby. This baby was Jesus, and His purpose was to surrender His life as a ransom for many people (Mark 10:45). The early Church grew expansively. What clues and tips can we take from them to help me? The Apostle Paul evangelised wherever people gathered together, such as at the Synagogue (Acts 18:4, 6) as well as in the marketplace or place of work (Acts 18:3, 13). Paul certainly had his fears, frustrations and limitations

Section B. The Armour We Wear

of his own weaknesses. However, he overcame them and used these experiences as a means to rely totally on God's power and strength. The same is indeed true for us today if we are honest with ourselves.

If that is where Paul shared the message, what are some of the various methods that he employed, which can help us as we seek to be obedient to the command of Jesus Christ? He reasoned from the Scriptures (Acts 18:3, 4 & 11) because Paul knew that Scripture had been revealed, inspired and illuminated by God. Paul knew that Scripture equipped for service. Paul knew that Scripture helped him get to know God more and that this was vital in order to be used in Evangelism. Paul knew that Scripture revealed God's programme and he was always prepared to change strategy (Acts 18:6). Paul was invited into homes of others (Acts 18:7) and he was careful to forge relationships (Acts 18:2, 7–8 & 17) with people.

Paul's Gospel message was "Jesus and Him crucified" (1 Corinthians 2:2). The Gospel is Jesus and that is why it is so central to the Gospel message. As important as the incarnation, crucifixion, resurrection and ascension are, the Gospel is Jesus. Not just a Jesus to whom anything can be attached, such as being a good friend, but the Jesus who was God–man, lived in this world, was falsely accused, condemned, crucified, died, rose again and ascended into heaven. In other words, the whole story of His life and death. At the very centre of that story, and most significant for us, was His death that secured our salvation and His resurrection which proved that He was the Messiah that He said He was.

> [6] This is the one who came by water and blood – Jesus Christ. He did not come by water only, but by water and blood. And it is the Spirit who testifies, because the Spirit is the truth. [7] For there are three that testify: [8] the Spirit, the water and the blood; and the three are in agreement. [9] We accept human testimony, but God's testimony is greater because it is the testimony of God, which He has given about His Son. [10] Whoever believes in

the Son of God accepts this testimony. Whoever does not believe God has made Him out to be a liar, because they have not believed the testimony God has given about His Son. [11] And this is the testimony: God has given us eternal life, and this life is in His Son. [12] Whoever has the Son has life; whoever does not have the Son of God does not have life. (1 John 5:9–12)

To all this, we can tell our own story of how Jesus has come into our lives and transformed us. One thing that all Christians have, regardless of who they are or where they are from, is a testimony, which is a story of how they became a follower of Jesus Christ. A testimony is an assertion offering first-hand authentication of a fact. For us, as Christians, our testimony is initially about how we came to be Christians, expresses why we are Christians, and what that means to us now. So a testimony is not just how but also why. Now, I could say that at as a teenager, I was invited along to a local youth group at the Baptist Church, and several weeks later, gave my life to Christ and became a Christian. That is, of course, partly true. The reason that I am a Christian is not because I chased God, but rather He chased me. Unknown to me at the time, God was chasing me and following my every path with the urgency of a lover after the beloved.

We are Christians, not because we attend Church services, or we that we happened to have been born in a supposedly Christian country. We are Christians entirely because God first chased and harried us into His arms. We are Christians, because God first loved us, and He beckoned and called us by name to respond to His call and follow Him. We are Christians not because of anything we have done, but rather because He first chased us, and because He first loved us. Jesus Himself said:

"For the Son of Man did not come to be served but to serve, and to give His life give His life as a ransom for many"
(Mark 10:45)

Section B. The Armour We Wear

We are Christians today, because of the joint events at Christmas and Easter when God entered this world as a human baby we know as Jesus Christ. He took all the necessary steps so that all people could have the choice to be His follower, His person, or not. In my smugger moments, I have been known to congratulate myself for being a Christian and that God was a jolly lucky God that I had decided to follow Him. It was during one of my less self–deluded moments that I examined myself and I found God the Holy Spirit, pricking my conscience and correcting me.

We read about the growth of the early church in the Book of Acts in the Bible. Christianity is a faith whereby all Christians, all followers of Jesus, are to tell others of the goodness of God. As followers of Jesus Christ, all we are to evangelize. Evangelism is showing and telling others of God's message of reconciliation to all people of all time. It is not forcing people to adopt Church standards (1 Corinthians 5:12) and nor is it simply a message of join the church as a symbol of good works (Ephesians 2:8–10). If people know you are a Christian, they will be watching how you behave, conduct yourself in your life and your words. You are a witness for God – whether you want to be or not. Let's be good witnesses. The prime motivation for evangelism is out of gratitude for what God has done, in that we love because He loved us first.

> "For Christ's love compels us, because we are convinced that one died for all, and therefore all died." As the servants and followers of Jesus, we are to tell and live out God's reconciling message – the message of Jesus Christ. (2 Corinthians 5:14)

We are all to do the work of an evangelist (2 Timothy 4:5) even though not everybody has the specific gift of being an evangelist. But we are not just to evangelise but also disciple. Intentionally make disciples of Jesus Christ. In the last words of Matthew's Gospel, all Christian Disciples are to make disciples throughout the whole earth:

> [18] Then Jesus came to them and said, 'All authority in heaven and on earth has been given to me. [19] Therefore go and make disciples of all nations, baptising them in the name of the Father and of the Son and of the Holy Spirit, [20] and teaching them to obey everything I have commanded you. And surely I am with you always, to the very end of the age.' (Matthew 28:18–20).

God the Holy Spirit is living within us, which is a constant reminder to us that it is by grace alone through faith alone, that we are children of the Living God. That is part of the message of Evangelism: people throughout the world, including the communities in which we live and work, can choose to become children of God. This is only by God's grace through faith alone. But if these people have never heard, how can they respond if the Church never tells them? As the Church today, corporately and individually, we have the imperative and the commandment to go and tell people the Good News of Jesus Christ.

We have feet fitted with the readiness that comes from the gospel of peace.

Section B. The Armour We Wear

Encouragement From Other Sojourners

What an acceptable work it is to win men to Christ! A doctor is never angry with a man who brings a patient to him, because through the cure his dedication and skill will be publicized. And this is the great design Christ has had for a long time, and prayed for – 'that the world may believe' that God sent Him (John 17:21). His aim in gathering in souls by the grace of the gospel is 'to take out … a people' from the heap of sinners 'for his name' (Acts 15:14) – to choose a peculiar people, show mercy on them and allow His glorious name to be exalted.[31]

We are not called upon to defend the whole of the Christian faith. No one man can do it at all points. Keep to familiar ground. Make sure that your feet are shod with 'the preparation of the gospel of peace'. You must be mobile, you must be free in every way and without encumbrances. … When will the Church wake up and realize that her strength lies not in her numbers but in her relationship to God, and her ability to respond to His every suggestion, His every stimulus, His every move. We must not be slow and heavy–footed.[32]

… the devil fears and hates the gospel, because it is God's power to rescue people from tyranny, both us who have received it and those with whom we share it.[33]

---

[31] Gurnall02, Page 304–305
[32] Lloyd–Jones01, Page 288
[33] Stott, Page 280

B4. Shield of Faith

²² Immediately Jesus made the disciples get into the boat and go on ahead of Him to the other side, while He dismissed the crowd. ²³ After He had dismissed them, He went up on a mountainside by Himself to pray. Later that night, He was there alone, ²⁴ and the boat was already a considerable distance from land, buffeted by the waves because the wind was against it.
²⁵ Shortly before dawn Jesus went out to them, walking on the lake. ²⁶ When the disciples saw Him walking on the lake, they were terrified. 'It's a ghost,' they said, and cried out in fear.
²⁷ But Jesus immediately said to them: 'Take courage! It is I. Don't be afraid.'
²⁸ 'Lord, if it's you,' Peter replied, 'tell me to come to you on the water.'
²⁹ 'Come,' He said.
Then Peter got down out of the boat, walked on the water and came towards Jesus. ³⁰ But when He saw the wind, He was afraid and, beginning to sink, cried out, 'Lord, save me!'
³¹ Immediately Jesus reached out His hand and caught Him. 'You of little faith,' He said, 'why did you doubt?'
³² And when they climbed into the boat, the wind died down. ³³ Then those who were in the boat worshipped Him, saying, 'Truly you are the Son of God.' (Matthew 14:22–33)

The common idea, indeed prevalent in the western worldview, is that faith, or belief, is one step down from knowledge. People talk about making the 'leap of faith'. Things that we know and are self–evident, are rock solid. Whereas things that we 'merely' believe without any form of evidence are not solid but rather they are things we just hope are true and right, but we cannot be absolutely sure of them. That may be true of some of the things we believe and have faith in, but it is

Section B. The Armour We Wear

certainly not true of Biblical faith. The Christian faith is founded on one solid fact: the resurrection of Jesus Christ from the dead. This is the on of the best–attested fact of ancient history. Yet many people feel they can doubt that it actually happened. Everybody accepts that Julius Caesar was assassinated in 44BC, yet the evidence of that event is far thinner than the evidence for the resurrection of Jesus.

Why the difference in attitude to the two events? The answer to that question is that many leaders have been assassinated down through the years, but the resurrection of Jesus was a once only event. Because the assassination was repeated it is accepted; because there has been only one resurrection, it is not acknowledged.

That argument is very understandable, but it is neither correct or right. It was in the very nature of the event, the salvation moment for all humanity, that it could never be repeated. It had to be a once and for all moment. But in order to prepare the people of that time, and everybody who has lived since, God carried out a series of events that teaches, step by step, that it was all completely possible. In particular, the redemption of the people from Egypt, over a thousand years earlier, teaches about redemption. The repeated sacrifices in the Jerusalem temple teaches about sacrifice. The lives of people such as Moses and David demonstrate what the life of a true person of God would look like. If the one event could not be repeated, it at least could be explained in advance and very carefully prepared for in great detail. It was not a completely strange event. Rather, it was only strange within its intensity, its force and its importance.

When we say that we have faith in the Lord Jesus or when we say we believe in the existence of God, we are therefore not operating on a lower level than when we say that we know the sun is behind the clouds even although we cannot see the sun. Ergo, we are placing our confidence in an event that happened a long time ago, but we can do so because the event is welded solidly into human history over many years, centuries and millennia.

What is faith? People say that faith is blind. The Bible, however, tells us that faith can be defined as a total confidence in God's faithfulness, which leads us in all aspects of life, to have complete reliance upon Him, trust in Him and show total obedience to Him (Hebrews 11:6). We see this faith in the Godly obedience of those around us who know Him, as well as hearing the testimonies and stories of those from the Bible and from Church history. To secure salvation, faith is a voluntary change of mind and heart in the sinner, whereby we turn to God, applying our own will to accepting God's offer of salvation through Jesus Christ, His Son. All parts of us are being transformed.

Firstly, there is our emotions or heart, and our personal assent to the gospel. We asked of ourselves, "What must we do to be saved?", whereby we agree to make salvation a prime part of our life. Secondly, our will, which is a personal trust in Jesus Christ. Lastly, our mind, in which we recognise our need of salvation and acknowledge Jesus Christ's death on our behalf and our need of forgiveness for those sins. As followers of Jesus, we are to continue having faith in Him. There are four things at least, we are to have faith in Him for.

By faith, Jesus Christ is praying for us. (Romans 8:34). He knew the troubles of the disciples (Mark 6:48), just as He knows our troubles now. He feels our cares and knowing what we are going through, encouraging us to continue to trust Him in all aspects of life because of His own experiences (Hebrews 4:14–16).

By faith, He will come to us. Have you ever felt as though God is far away? Well, we have before now, and we are not alone in thinking such things at times. King David often felt that God was far away and unconcerned about what He was undergoing (Psalm 22:1–21). However, King David also knew that God would ultimately rescue Him (Psalm 22:22–31). Jesus always comes to us through difficult times, although He may not come in the time that we think He should come. We trust Jesus because He knows when we need Him most and will come then. King David often felt God was far away and unconcerned.

Section B. The Armour We Wear

However he also knew God would ultimately rescue Him. Paul, the great Apostle, also felt himself to be under pressure:

> "[8] We do not want you to be uninformed, brothers and sisters, about the troubles we experienced in the province of Asia. We were under great pressure, far beyond our ability to endure, so that we despaired of life itself." (2 Corinthians 1:8)

By faith, Jesus will help us grow. One time the disciples were in boat on the stormy sea and Jesus came to them walking on the water (Matthew 14:25). The purpose of that incident was to show that they had to learn to trust in Him when He wasn't physically present since He would be soon leaving them. Perhaps this is what Peter was thinking of when later on in His life, he quotes the Psalmist (Psalm 24:16):

> For the eyes of the Lord are on the righteous and His ears are attentive to their prayer, but the face of the Lord is against those who do evil." (1 Peter 3:12)

By faith, therefore, God will see us through all things. He has done so for us in the past and He will do so again in the future. Jesus said to Peter, "Come" and Peter went to Jesus walking on the water (Matthew 14:29). This must have encouraged the other disciples, for when they saw Jesus' power, they worshipped Him. Whatever troubles we are undergoing are temporary, and Jesus will see us through.

By faith, we have salvation. By faith Jesus is praying for us, will come to us, grow us and help us through our concerns, worries and troubles, regardless of what they may be. By being obedient to God, we are showing our salvation to other people. We are showing that faith is not blind and inert as some propose, but rather we display that faith is dynamic and active. We hold fast and upright, the shield of faith.

Through, and by faith, we persevere. This is the perseverance in relation to God and His work, which is the continuous operation of the Holy Spirit in our life as Christians believer. It is a work of divine grace that is begun in our heart when we became Christians, and which will be continued with and brought to completion. Because of God's perseverance and His complete and utter reliability, our faith and we will never perish, and nobody can snatch us out of His hand (John 10:27–29). The good work that God began in us, will be carried on to completion (Philippians 1:6), as we are shielded by God's almighty power (1 Peter 1:5). We hold onto the fact that nobody or nothing can separate us from the love of God that is in Christ Jesus, our Lord (Romans 8:38–39). We persevere in faith, based on the fact that Jesus Christ knows those who are His people (2 Timothy 2:19).

Our eternal life never depends on our own feeble grip on Jesus Christ, but rather on His firm grip upon us, as we are fulfilling God's purpose of transforming us into the very image of His Son, Jesus. This is where perseverance for us as Christians comes in. Through faith, we persevere by keeping our eyes focussed on Jesus Christ throughout each day and being obedient to Him. As followers of Jesus, we persevere in faith with our relationship with God. This is evidenced as we obey Him and follow Him closely, asking Him questions humbly and expecting Him to answer. Particularly if we don't understand something. By faith, God will persevere with us, turning us gradually into the image of His Son, Jesus Christ.

We hold firmly, in His strength, to the shield of faith.

Section B. The Armour We Wear

Encouragement From Other Sojourners

… not only does the shield defend the whole body, but it defends the soldier's other armour also. It keeps the arrow from the helmet as well as from the head, from both breast and breastplate alike. Thus faith is armour upon armour, a grace that preserves all the other graces.[34]

The holding up of the shield of faith reminds you that you are looking to God the Father, God the Son, and God the Holy Spirit. It means that you are depending upon God and His grace in Christ. It means that you link yourself in your mind and thought to Him who has all power, and will enable us to be 'more than conquerors'.[35]

Faith is the Christian's shield. The devil can do nothing against it. His worst attacks are frustrated. Faith offers complete protection and makes advance possible. Where there is faith, there is nothing to fear. And what is faith? It is taking God at His word. It is accepting His teaching, obeying His commands, heeding His threats and laying hold of His promises. Where there is faith, defeat is unknown.[36]

God's protection is to ensure that we get to our destination safely: He doesn't just 'put us on the bus' and then leave it up to us.[37]

---

[34] Gurnall03, Page 30
[35] Lloyd-Jones01, Page 308
[36] Olyott, Page 138
[37] Whitman, Page 27

B5. Helmet of Salvation

> "My dear friends, as you have always obeyed—not only in my presence, but now much more in my absence—continue to work out your salvation with fear and trembling, for it is God who works in you to will and to act in order to fulfil His good purpose." (Philippians 2:12–13)

Salvation means 'a rescue' or 'having been saved'. As humans, when we were born, we inherited that sinful nature we looked at earlier and were subsequently alienated from God. But God has seen fit to offer a way back into relationship with Him, so that we may no longer be alienated from Him. This offer of relationship is a result of Jesus, who was both fully God and fully human, dying on the cross at Calvary. We are saved because this is an act of salvation, which is available for all people of all time and of every nation. As Christians, we have accepted the offer and we are to live so as to please God alone as a priority above our own self or of that of anybody else.

The question "Who decides the saved?" has been asked for centuries. There are two extremist views – one view states "God has decided all things, and nothing can be done about it." The other view is, "universalism", which states that God will grant salvation to all, regardless of creed, race or religion. But we need to see these two views in the balance of Scripture.

Firstly, God does choose individuals to fulfil His purposes (Romans 9) and He chooses those who are, or will be, saved (John 15:16). These chosen ones are called the elect. However, it is also equally true, that it is His will that all people should be saved (1 Timothy 2:3–4) and that nobody should perish (2 Peter 3:9). Therefore, we must accept that both these Scriptural statements are equally and absolutely true. When we use words concerning God that have a time element attached, such as 'chose' or 'elect', we need to consider God's infinite time framework and

Section B. The Armour We Wear

His timelessness. God does not work in our human finite time framework. As Christians, we are now saved from everlasting alienation from Him, for that is what hell is. Instead, we are saved into an everlasting relationship with Him, for that is what heaven is.

One day, as Christians, we will die and be with Jesus, who is our Lord, our King, our Saviour and our friend. We will be with for eternity in a place we know as heaven. What is this place of heaven like? People, both believers and non–believers have an opinion about heaven. To many people, heaven is where everybody will meet up after death, providing that they were not too bad in this earthly life. The caricature of the comedians is that in heaven, everybody not exceedingly bad, will be floating around on clouds and playing a harp. What does the Bible, have to say about heaven?

The first thing to say is that heaven is a physical place with the physical properties as a house (John 14:2), a Kingdom (Matthew 25:34), paradise (2 Corinthians 12:2–4) and a Holy City (Revelation 21:2). Heaven is part of the inheritance of all Christians. (1 Peter 1:4). Heaven is a place replete with glory (Romans 8:17–18), joy (Luke 15:7–10), peace (Luke 16:19–25), reward (Matthew 5:11–12), rest (Revelation 14:13), righteousness (2 Peter 3:13) and service (Revelation 7:15). No sitting around on clouds there! For instance, service implies working.

Who is it prepared for and who can enter heaven? It is for all those recorded in the Book of Life (Malachi 3:16–18, Philippians 4:3; Revelation 20:12). As we have salvation and that God has declared us to be righteous (Matthew 5:20), and holy (Revelation 19:8), we will be seen amongst the obedient (Revelation 22:14).

We will enter heaven through giant gates of pearl (Revelation 21:21). A pearl is formed as an oyster suffers, covering a grain of irritating sand, until the irritation ceases. Now what do you think the suffering was, that created these giant pearls that are the gates? It can only be the cross of Jesus Christ and the incredible suffering and pain that He endured upon it. Only through the pain, the agony and the suffering that Jesus endured, culminating in His death as He cried out "My God! Our God! Why have you forsaken me?" (Matthew 27:46). It is only through the death of Jesus on the cross that we can be declared holy and righteous. Only those who have been declared as such will be able to be in the presence of Almighty God. Those who have been declared holy, are only those who have embraced Jesus Christ during their earthly life and followed Him. As Christians, our current attitude towards heaven should be to desire it (2 Corinthians 5:2–8), eagerly keep watch for it (2 Peter 3:13) and to put our treasure there (Luke 12:32–34). Heaven is a prepared place and it is perfect. Jesus Himself promised:

> [1] 'Do not let your hearts be troubled. You believe in God; believe also in me. [2] My Father's house has many rooms; if that were not so, would I have told you that I am going there to prepare a place for you? [3] And if I go and prepare a place for you, I will come back and take you to be with me that you also may be where I am. [4] You know the way to the place where I am going.' (John 14:1–4)

God the Son, Jesus Christ, has prepared a place for those who love Him, trust Him and obey Him as King.

> [1] Then I saw 'a new heaven and a new earth,' for the first heaven and the first earth had passed away, and there was no longer any sea. [2] I saw the Holy City, the new Jerusalem, coming down out of heaven from God, prepared as a bride beautifully dressed for her husband. [3] And I heard a loud voice from the throne saying, 'Look! God's dwelling–place is now among the people, and He will dwell with them. They will be His people, and God Himself will be with them and be their God. [4] "He will wipe every tear from their eyes. There will be no more death" or mourning or crying or pain, for the old order of things has passed away.' (Revelation 21:1–4)

Section B. The Armour We Wear

From this picture given by John, Heaven is also a pure place. In this earthly life, every human suffers in some way. We know that we have in the past, we do currently and will in the future. When our King returns, man's inhumanity to man will no longer be allowed. One day, there will be no more pain, death, suffering and sin. Perfection will be reached, and it is to the glory of an Almighty and merciful God, that this will occur.

Two words of gentle warning though. Firstly, all that, is describing the indescribable, in human terms. For the simple reason there is no other way to do it. So, therefore, we need to be careful at how literally we take it.

Secondly, it seems that it is not heaven that is our destination, but the new heavens and the new, that is revived, earth (Romans 8:22–25; Revelation 21:1). How those two interlock is not at all clear and, it quite possibly serves as a deliberate reminder that we should be cautious as we look down the tunnel of time to the light at the far end.

At Christmas, we celebrate Jesus Christ coming to earth as a human. Christmas is a time where the Church and our community celebrate Jesus Christ's first coming as a baby. The community like to think of Jesus as a baby, because a baby can be controlled, to a degree. Society in general, is comfortable with leaving Jesus as a baby. However, Jesus is not a baby now. Jesus is King and what a King. He has promised that He is coming again, not as a baby, but as King and judge.

When I go away from home by myself, I know that when I get home, I know I am expected and loved. My wife has my favourite meal prepared. Everything I like, that makes it a home for me, is done for me! Similarly, when we Christians get to heaven, Jesus has prepared a place for all who love Him, trust Him and obey Him as King. Our King is waiting for us! He is expecting us, wanting to lavish His love upon us. We know He loves us now, but that is only in part. When we are with Him eternally, we shall have the full picture of Jesus. He is with us now in Spirit, but then we shall be with Him physically and face to face.

Heaven is a prepared place of majestic beauty. The Apostle John portrays his visions, building up layer upon layer of words, just as an artist does when painting a painting, laying on the colours, layer upon layer until finally the painting is finished.

One glorious day, all suffering will be banished for those who love Jesus now and He will wipe the tears from our eyes, as He takes our face in His hands (Revelation 21:4). What a glorious day it will be for those who like us, love God now. God Himself, with our face in His hands, wiping away our tears. It will be a place where we will live the fruit of the spirit eternally. It will be an amazing place where the fruit of the Spirit, "love, joy, peace, longsuffering, kindness, goodness, faithfulness, gentleness and self–control" (Galatians 5:22–23) are both permanent and universal.

That is part of the manifesto of Jesus, our King. What a wondrous and glorious day that will be! We will enter those gates, thanking Jesus. We will be able to say with other Christian believers, "It was worth it all." Heaven is prepared for us, and it is a pure place. Our King Himself has suffered for us, so that we may enjoy His company forever and ever, if we only trust and obey Him now and place our faith in Him while we are here in this our temporal home on earth. We know in part now, but then we will know in full.

This makes the sins that we commit while we are here on earth as we follow Jesus, even more serious. Sometimes we take a rather blasé attitude to sin. We excuse them as only a minor thing and of no consequence. Each time we sin as a believer, it is as if we are spitting in the very face of Jesus. Our desire should be, to be Jesus and to be like Him. We long to be perfect. When we make a mistake and sin, we cry out in frustration to be perfect now!

However, we also know that God is smoothing our rough edges to continue making us purer, more like His Son and our King, under the power and direction of the Holy Spirit. We can only enter heaven, our new home, through the cross of Jesus Christ. When we first decided for

Section B. The Armour We Wear

Jesus and turned over our lives to Him, that is when our eternal life with Him commenced. Heaven is our home and one day we will be with our King forever. In the meantime, when we sin, we are to keep a short account and ask for forgiveness as soon as we recognise that we have sinned, and the Holy Spirit has convicted us of it. We yearn to be with our King for ever and ever. Yet, we are to keep one part of our mind on Heaven and the other on the responsible work we have been set to do, here on earth. We are not to be so heavenly minded, that we are of no earthly use. We are also not to be so earth bound, that we are not tied to King Jesus in our eternal home. We are to go and tell others about Jesus. Heaven is a great big place, and there will be room for everybody to enter through one of those twelve gates!

Jesus Christ is our King of Righteousness. We are to fully trust Him and live a life worthy of Him, while looking for His coming back again! We are to be expectant, for our King is coming back for us soon! He has promised and He will do it! Jesus is completely and utter dependable, reliable and worthy of our trust in Him. Our God, our King Jesus, will appear soon. He is coming back as the King of Righteousness, in order to judge evil and reject those who reject Him whilst rewarding those who patiently trust and obey Him. Which camp are you in?

> [7] Then war broke out in heaven. Michael and his angels fought against the dragon, and the dragon and his angels fought back. [8] But he was not strong enough, and they lost their place in heaven. [9] The great dragon was hurled down – that ancient snake called the devil, or Satan, who leads the whole world astray. He was hurled to the earth, and his angels with him.
> [10] Then I heard a loud voice in heaven say:
> 'Now have come the salvation and the power and the kingdom of our God, and the authority of his Messiah.
> For the accuser of our brothers and sisters,
> who accuses them before our God day and night,
> has been hurled down. (Revelation 12:7–10)

Engaged in Battle

The great enemy, Satan, is defeated, he is beaten, and he will no longer be any threat. Same with other adversaries, our old nature and sin. All because of Jesus Christ, the Son of God. As we are engaged in battle, we persevere in the power of the Holy Spirit. In His strength, we overcome all adversaries, knowing that Jesus is King, that we are His, He has called us by name to follow Him and He is coming back for us because He loves us.

We can echo the words of the Apostle John, whom Jesus loved: "Come, Lord Jesus!" (Revelation 22:20)

We can only praise God for this and await that day. Knowing that we have been saved by God alone. We are saved by and through God alone and we will be saved due to God alone, from His wellsprings of grace and mercy. We have been, are, and will be saved to a life living with God. All because of Jesus Christ. To follow Jesus Christ is to participate in salvation. We are saved. We are being saved. We will be saved. The three great tenses of salvation.

We wear the helmet of salvation.

Section B. The Armour We Wear

Encouragement From Other Sojourners

Do you have a sin which refuses to bow? Has the lust for money snared you? Let your hope of heaven be strong enough to charm this devil! Can gold control you when you hope to be an heir of that city where gold has no price? That place is paved with gold; God says we will walk on it. Will you let gold lie in your heart now when some day it will be under your feet?[38]

The helmet protects the head, which next to the hear is the most vulnerable point in man. Salvation, known, realized, enjoyed and worked out in practice, is that helmet for us.[39]

Believers are destined to be absolutely perfect, free from sin, from all vestiges of evil, 'without spot, wrinkle, or any such thing'. We shall be glorified, we shall be like Christ, we shall see Him as He is and be like Him; our bodies shall be changed, we shall be completely glorified – saved entirely, body, soul and spirit; with nothing lacking. That is the hope! And putting on the helmet of salvation means realizing that that is coming.[40]

Raised from the dead, acquitted at the final judgement, we shall spend eternity in the new heavens and earth. There, in perfect holiness and happiness, we shall fully enjoy God for ever.[41]

---

[38] Gurnall03, Page 166
[39] Hole, Page 63
[40] Lloyd-Jones01, Page 320
[41] Olyott, Page 138

B6. Sword of the Spirit

Another weapon of spiritual warfare, is the sword of the Spirit. This is God's Word, the Bible, which is the primary way by which we hear God speak. I personally have only heard God's voice audibly once. That occurred back in 2007 when I collapsed in the GP surgery and while unconscious, I said "Dad, can I come home now?" At which point, God said "No. Get up. I have a job for you to do." So I sat up and the attending paramedics almost fainted!

However, God does speak through the Bible, His written word. Throughout the Bible God is revealed, whereby He makes Himself known to all sorts of people from all kinds of backgrounds. People are not naturally born possessing this knowledge, even though they know God's very existence. Knowing that God exists is different from actually knowing God personally.

Personal knowledge of God is ultimately crucial however, since knowing God personally and developing the relationship is what being Christians is all about. As Christians, we should be rejoicing that God earnestly desires us to attain this knowledge of Him, in order to know Him more and more. For this reason, He has spoken to us through His Word, the Bible, revealing Himself and disclosing how we may know Him more.

Whilst God can be known, our knowledge of God is partial, and we will never know everything there is to be known about Him. Knowledge of Him is both wondrous and without end. As we grow spiritually, knowing the Bible and thus knowing Him more, we will grow in spiritual maturity. The Apostle Peter commands that we grow in the knowledge of Jesus (2 Peter 3:18). We do this as part of our spiritual journey in order to become more like Jesus. One of the Christian life's' greatest delights, is developing an intimate knowledge of God and relationship with Him. The gospel, or the good news of Jesus Christ, which we share with others, is entitled 'the power of God

Section B. The Armour We Wear

to salvation'. The Bible, and its gospel by which people come to know God, is the agent of the new birth. It is the soap or cleansing agent whereby God gives the believing sinner a spiritual bath resulting in salvation. The Bible is a teacher that brings wisdom which leads to salvation.

As Christians, we believe that God has spoken to this world because He loves this world. The Apostle John tells us that God is love (1 John 4:16). An inherent part of love is a desire to both know and to be known. One aspect of that love is the reason as to why God became man in Jesus Christ, because God wanted to know and be known in the fullest, human way possible. Another aspect of God's love is the reason the prophets spoke, history was recorded, and the Bible was therefore written. God wanted His message to be given to all people. But what are Christians to believe about the Bible?

There are three words which summarize what Christians are to believe about the Bible. It is God's revealed word about His Son Jesus Christ, which is inspired by His Holy Spirit and illuminated within us as we seek Him. What do we mean when we say God has spoken to the world using those three methods through the Bible? Revelation, whereby God has caused the truth to be revealed. Inspiration since God has caused the truth to be recorded. Finally, Illumination where God causes the truth to be understood.

The Bible, as God's written word, is revelation. Revelation is how God has communicated truths to people, who otherwise would not know them. The story of creation in Genesis 1 and 2 is a good example of this. As humanity was not created until the sixth day, it must have been God who revealed the knowledge about what occurred on the first five days to the author of Genesis, or it would not be possible to know what occurred. We know God spoke to those who wrote the Bible, but how did He speak? We know that He spoke to them in their own language, just as He did to young Samuel in the temple. Samuel at first thought that the voice was that of Eli the priest (1 Samuel 3:3–9). At other times God spoke through angels, as when the angel Gabriel informed Mary that she would give birth to Jesus (Luke 1:26–38). In the Old Testament, God often spoke through the "Angel of the Lord" (Judges 2:4; Zechariah 1:12). Some people believe this to have been Jesus before He came to earth as a human (Joshua 5:13–15; 1 Chronicles 21:16). These events are called a 'christophany', which is a pre-incarnate appearance of Jesus the Son of God.

God also communicated in dreams and visions. An example of this is in the birth story of Jesus Christ, where the wise men were warned in a dream not to return to King Herod (Matthew 2:12). God has also communicated from a burning bush (Exodus 3) and from within a cloud (Exodus 34). God has even spoken through a donkey, as the prophet Balaam can testify (Numbers 22). Without revelation, we could not learn about God. Unless God reveals Himself, we would not know anything about Him. As Solomon stated:

> "He (God) has also set eternity in the human heart; yet no one can fathom what God has done from beginning to end." (Ecclesiastes 3:11)

I know for certain that this revelation has caused the Bible, the Written Word of God, to reveal Jesus Christ, the Living Word of God.

GOD SPEAKS BY INSPIRATION

As Christians, we also believe the Bible is inspired. But what do we mean by that? The actual word 'inspiration' is found only once in the New Testament, when Paul explicitly states, "All Scripture is given by inspiration of God" or more literally "All Scripture is God–breathed" (2 Timothy 3:16). The word 'inspiration' is actually not the best translation. The original Greek word says God 'breathed out' His Word. Divine inspiration naturally proceeds from divine revelation. While through revelation God speaks to humanity, it is by inspiration that

God works the pen, ergo ensuring that the message is God breathed and written correctly. This process of inspiration has a number of theories attached to it. One theory called the content theory, suggests that the author was given the main idea by God, but God allowed the writer to choose their own words.

Another is the natural theory. This is where the Biblical writers were inspired in the same sense Shakespeare was inspired, but that doesn't agree with the 'God–breathed' word. It is quite apparent that God did not suppress the writers' personalities. For example, the writing style of John is clearly different from that of Peter or indeed that of Paul. The differences in writing style and in vocabulary of different authors are easily seen.

However, Jesus implied clearly that God chose the very letters of the words when He said that not one stroke of the pen would pass from the law (Matthew 5:17–19). From this, we can infer that God inspires all the words of the Bible. God wanted to communicate to ordinary people, therefore He used ordinary people to write and produce the Bible.

In response to temptation by Satan, Jesus said that humanity is to live by God's inspired words (Matthew 4:4, 7 & 10). Writers in the Bible, such as Peter, knew their writings were being guided by God (1 Peter 1:10–12; 2 Peter 1:19–20, 3:15–16). Inspiration is only guaranteed in the original manuscripts which were written in Hebrew, Greek or Aramaic. It is not, however much some people protest, guaranteed in any translation of the Bible.

GOD SPEAKS BY ILLUMINATION

God has spoken and He has communicated His Written Word to humanity. Firstly, by revelation when God spoke to the writers. Secondly, through inspiration, as God divinely guided the writers, in the process of writing His message. However, in order to understand God's revealed and inspired message, illumination is required. This is where God causes the Bible to be understood by both the human heart and the mind.

Without illumination, we continue to be blinded both by our own old nature and by Satan. Just as a light bulb needs power in order to give light, so the Bible needs somebody to provide the power. The person, who does this illuminating, is God the Holy Spirit. Jesus promised that the Holy Spirit would illuminate the Bible to the hearts and minds of all those people willing to listen, both Christian and non–Christian.

Take for example the event recorded in Acts 2. This is where the Holy Spirit uses God's Word to illuminate sinners at Pentecost, where after hearing Peter preach, over three thousand people became Christians (Acts 2:41).

As Christians, we also need this illumination to help us to understand the Bible. The Holy Spirit will reveal truths to us as we read the Bible regularly, asking for His help in understanding it. God's Living Word Jesus Christ is revealed as the Holy Spirit illuminates the Bible as God's inspired written word. That way people's lives are transformed and changed. Therefore, we continue to pray for His help and illumination when reading the Bible, God's written Word.

We hold fast the sword of the Spirit, which is the Bible, God's written Word which reveals God's Living Word, Jesus Christ.

Section B. The Armour We Wear

Encouragement From Other Sojourners

The sword is the weapon continually used by soldiers to defend themselves and to rout their enemies. Thus it illustrates the most excellent use of God's Word, but which the believer both defends himself and cuts down his enemies.[42]

God is preparing us for Himself, and the ultimate end of salvation is that we go with God and enjoy God's life with Him. What poor creatures we are, what foolish creatures, grumbling and complaining, holding on to His world. Do you know that you and I, if we are in Christ, are destined to enjoy the life and the glory of God Himself. That is the glory that awaits us.[43]

The devil cannot stand against the Holy Spirit working through the Scriptures. It is by the proclamation of God's Word that minds are enlightened, lives are changed and conversions take place. Spiritual work is done by spiritual weaponry.[44]

Of all the six pieces of the armour or weaponry listed, the sword is the only one which can clearly be used for attack as well as defence. Moreover, the kind of attack envisaged will involve a close personal encounter, for the word used is *machaira*, the short sword.[45]

---

[42] Gurnall03, Page 244–245
[43] Lloyd–Jones02, Page 105
[44] Olyott, Page 139
[45] Stott, Page 282

Section C: Weapon of Memory

The ability to remember is a wonderful gift of God to us all. Memories can bring about the full gamut of emotions: sadness, bitterness, anger, joy and ecstasy! My memory often fails. Sometimes I will think I have remembered something, but it turns out to be a false memory of an event that never occurred. Other times I will forget to remember something, and then miss something important. There maybe even be occasions in this little book where I have repeated myself because I have forgotten it was already written! Forgive me if you notice them.

Throughout the Old Testament, Israel were to be a light to the nations, set apart by God, for God, in this world, to go out into the world. One of the reasons that the rules and laws of Leviticus were there, was so that other nations and peoples could see that the nation of Israel was entirely different to them in all manner of life and ways. To enable this to be done, they were often told to use their memory. For example, they were told often to remember their God (Exodus 3:15), all that He had done for them (Deuteronomy 4:20) and all that they were to do as His called out nation to the world (Exodus 12:24).

The role of memory is key in our spiritual battle and it is one of the weapons in our arsenal of warfare. By remembering certain things, we are helped to live our whole life for Jesus. One of the reasons why we succumb to Satan and sin, is because we quite readily forget who our God is and what He has done for us. We forget who we are as Christians. We can remind ourselves, as well as other Christians, of these things, which helps us to behave rightly as followers of Jesus Christ, and to live a life which is honouring to Him. We can be reminded of the assurance of our salvation, which can only be brought about by being in a living and dynamic relationship with God. This helps us to be assured that we are indeed His beloved children, and it helps us to lean on Him, into Him and overcome our adversaries as we are engaged in spiritual warfare. Let's go. Let's remember.

Section C: Weapon of Memory

C1. We March In God's Victory

The first thing we remember is to put our spiritual armour on. How is this done? We don't put it our spiritual armour on through some mystical, deep and secret process. If it were, then we probably wouldn't wear it. The armour is revealed upon us, whenever we resist our adversaries and ignore the temptations they place before us. For example, when our marriages reflect the sacrificial love that Jesus has for the Church, our spiritual armour is displayed.

When we are sharing the Gospel and instructing others in the truth, our spiritual armour is being worn. When God is glorified in our life, we are wearing the spiritual armour. When we are living a fruitful life for God alone and giving all glory and honour to Him without compromise, we show that we are wearing our spiritual armour. We can stand up for Jesus and say with honesty and integrity that He is our Lord and our Master. When we meditate on God's word, we nourish our mind with the truth of salvation. When we tell others of this message of peace with God, our enemies flee. When we ask others to pray for us, as Paul did, we show that we are part of the beautiful bride of Jesus, which is the Church (Romans 15:30–32; Ephesians 6:18–20; 1 Thessalonians 5:25).

We remember that it as we are engaged in battle, that this battle has already been won by God and the victory is His. We are marching with Him! It is easy to forget this, particularly when we are in the midst of trouble and turmoil, being faced down by our adversaries.

Jesus Christ started His public ministry at His baptism, during which, He was revealed as God's Son (Luke 3:21–23). That must have been an amazing scene to witness. Not only was Jesus fully God, but He was also simultaneously fully human. In the other synoptic Gospel accounts of this event, Matthew and Mark write that Jesus was led by the Holy Spirit into the desert (Matthew 4:1; Mark 1:12). This is confirmed by Luke when he writes:

Engaged in Battle

> ¹ Jesus, full of the Holy Spirit, left the Jordan and was led by the Spirit into the wilderness, ² where for forty days He was tempted by the devil. He ate nothing during those days, and at the end of them He was hungry. (Luke 4:1–2)

Luke's phrasing and terminology makes it abundantly clear that Jesus' temptation experiences in the desert were all part of God's plan at the start of Jesus' public ministry. He did this in order to reveal the type of Messiah that Jesus was and would be. This temptations event reveals Jesus' perfect and full humanity. Knowing that Jesus was indeed, both fully God and fully man, Satan starts his plan of attack against Him. After forty days of fasting, prayer and wandering in the desert, Jesus is confronted by Satan. In this event, Jesus undergoes three different temptations. This also reveals the way that we as Christians should also handle temptations when confronted with them.

> ³ the devil said to Him, 'if you are the son of god, tell this stone to become bread.'
>
> ⁴ Jesus answered, 'It is written: "man shall not live on bread alone." (Luke 4:3–4)

Note the way Satan starts when he says, "So you are the Son of God." It is as if Satan was really saying: "If you are really who those voices speaking at your baptism say you are, then prove it to us. Prove it to us now. You must surely be hungry by now! Why don't you turn these stones into bread and feed yourself?" Satan wanted Jesus to use His powers for selfish purposes and therefore be disobedient to God the Father's will. Satan also wanted Jesus to doubt God the Father's personal love and care of Him. Jesus, however, is the beloved Son of God who always does the will of God the Father, His Father (John 8:29). Jesus answered Satan by referring back to Scripture itself (Luke 4:4):

> "man does not live on bread alone but on every word that comes from the mouth of the LORD." (Deuteronomy 8:3)

Section C: Weapon of Memory

This discloses that while physical food is necessary, it is more important to be sustained by the authority of Scripture. For Jesus, instead of relying on His own power to create food, it demonstrated His total and perfect trust in God the Father to take care of Him by supplying His needs. You would be forgiven for thinking that Satan would stop there but no, he continues in his wiles and scheme against Jesus. Satan continues because he knows that Jesus really is the Son of God and that Jesus is the only hope of the world.

> [5] The devil led Him up to a high place and showed Him in an instant all the kingdoms of the world. [6] And He said to Him, "I will give you all their authority and splendour; it has been given to me, and I can give it to anyone I want to. [7] If you worship me, it will all be yours."
>
> [8] Jesus answered, "It is written: 'Worship the Lord your God and serve Him only.' (Luke 4:5–8)

This is Satan's encouragement for Jesus to engage in false worship, as he challenges Jesus to break the commandment which forbids all forms of idolatry:

> "You shall have no other gods before me. (Exodus 20:3)

Satan says "It can all be yours, Jesus, if only you just bow the knee and worship us." Of course, Satan is, as always, telling a deceiving half–truth. Though Satan has great power (John 12:31), he has neither the power nor the authority to be able to offer Jesus everything that he said that he would give. Satan is also not worthy of worship, as his power is always destructive and leads to wanton disobedience and unfaithfulness.

This reflects Satan's self–delusion of hideous grandeur. Jesus' reply, is naturally to quote Scripture back at Satan:

> "Fear the LORD your God, serve Him only and take your oaths in His name." (Deuteronomy 6:13)

Engaged in Battle

Jesus is saying that He will only serve one Master, and that is God alone. Satan still continues with his wiles and perseveres regardless.

> [9] The devil led Him to Jerusalem and had Him stand on the highest point of the temple. "If you are the Son of God," He said, "throw yourself down from here. [10] For it is written:
>
> "'He will command His angels concerning you to guard you carefully; [11] they will lift you up in their hands,
>
> so that you will not strike your foot against a stone.'"
>
> [12] Jesus answered, "It is said: 'Do not put the Lord your God to the test.'"
>
> [13] When the devil had finished all this tempting, He left Him until an opportune time. (Luke 4:9–13)

In this temptation, Satan encourages Jesus to take God the Father up on His promised protection. Satan tauntingly says "Throw yourself off the top of the temple. If God is faithful and true, God will catch you and protect you as you start off on this supposed ministry of yours." Satan here is quoting Scripture to make the temptation seem somehow much more appealing to Jesus (Psalm 91:11–12). However, this is misquoted, because Satan doesn't use "in all your ways" from the original. Jesus however, being always wise, quotes Scripture back:

"Do not put the Lord your God to the test." (Deuteronomy 6:16)

Jesus, in quoting Scripture back to Satan, gives balance to the total expression of God's will, and not just to part of that will. Jesus refused to acquiesce to the lures of Satan and his demands to test God the Father's faithfulness. Jesus emerged from this incident as the victor and went on to continue His ministry. Satan crept away for the next opportunity to tempt Jesus.

As Christians, we need to be aware of the schemes of Satan, and learn to fend him off, just as Jesus did during His earthly ministry. What can we learn from this encounter to help us in our daily Christian life?

Section C: Weapon of Memory

We see that the first temptation is echoed within us when we try to do things in our own strength and power instead of relying on God's power and strength to achieve much more than we can hope for or imagine.

The second temptation here is echoed by James where desires and lusts attempt to lure us into sinning against God and disobeying Him (James 1:14–15).

The third temptation occurs when we actively disobey God, subsequently falling into trouble and then expect God to rescue us. That is a sin of testing God.

How are we, therefore, as Christians, to deal with Satan and temptation? We need to stay with the faith (1 Peter 5:9). How can we do this? We can overcome temptation to sin by doing the following. While recognising Satan's power and deception (2 Corinthians 2:11; Ephesians 6:11), we are not to give him the opportunities to tempt and accuse us (Ephesians 4:27). By openly resisting him by submitting solely and quickly to God, we know that Satan must flee (James 4:7). Lastly, which we will explore in more detail in the next section, we are to ensure that we are clad in the armour of God (Ephesians 6:10–17).

As we grow and mature as Christians, we continue growing more in love with God, our intimacy with Him is strengthened and therefore our desire to commit sin grows less. Our commitment to God continues to intensify. By having faith and trust in God to provide needs and protection. Through worshipping and serving Him alone, we grow in spiritual maturity and will also not succumb to temptation to sin and disobey God. These are the adversaries that we have to face as Christian believers and disciples. Jesus, the Lord of the Church, our Lord, also faced these adversaries and defeated them.

The combination of Jesus Christ's death on the cross and His subsequent resurrection from death to new life, results in forgiveness of sins and salvation being only found in and through Jesus Christ. This was the major motivation in the early Church evangelism (Acts 2:32,

Romans 4:24–25). Jesus' resurrection is a sign of the bodily resurrection for all believers in Him, giving a new attitude to death and transforming hopes (Romans 8:10; 1 Corinthians 15:12–58; 2 Corinthians 4:14; 1 Peter 1:3, 21). As the resurrected King, Jesus now intercedes for us and He has perfected our redemption as well as that of all those who choose to follow Him (Romans 5:10; Hebrews 6:20; 1 Peter 1:21).

Finally, the death and resurrection of Jesus Christ, ensures victory over Satan, sin and death – they are conquered and squashed. Satan is a defeated creature and will do anything to drag people into defeat with him. The powers of Satan, sin and death are conquered, and their grip upon each person is overcome, if that person is a Christian, a believer in Jesus Christ. The grip of Satan, sin and death upon us as Christians is no more because Jesus, the Son of God, has His grip upon us. Satan, the arch accuser, can no longer accuse us as Christians in the presence of God. Death also has been beaten, because those who believe and trust in Jesus Christ will live forever with Him. Death is not the end but a beginning. One day we shall be with Jesus, the very Son of God who is the King of Kings and Lord of Lords, forevermore. We are not marching to victory, but rather marching with victory, as victorious sojourners, because victory has already been achieved by King Jesus through His death and resurrection. Until that great day though when we are with our King forever, we take and live out that message every day. In the meantime, we are to be prepared daily as we encounter our adversaries.

Section C: Weapon of Memory

Encouragement From Other Sojourners

Knowing all that was to happen, Jesus went forth and said "Whom seek ye?" (John 18:4). Satan could not overcome Him – our Saviour never lost a battle, not even when He lost His life. He won the victory, carrying His spoils to heaven in the triumphant chariot of His ascension.[46]

The Holy Scriptures, especially St Paul, everywhere ascribe unto Christ that which He gives to the Father, namely, the divine almighty power; so that He can give grace, and peace of conscience, forgiveness of sins, life, victory over sin, and death, and the devil.[47]

Only the power of God can defend and deliver us from the might, the evil and craft of the devil. True, the principalities and powers are strong, but the power of God is stronger. It is His power which raised Jesus Christ from the dead and enthroned him in the heavenly places, and which has raised us from the death of sin and enthroned us with Christ.[48]

Christ has won the victory for us. We are to stand firm in it, proclaim it and rejoice in it. That is the way to resist Satan.[49]

---

[46] Gurnall01, Page 26–27
[47] Luther, Page 105
[48] Stott, Page 266
[49] Watson, Page 181

C2. We Abide With God

¹⁰ Finally, be strong in the Lord and in His mighty power.
(Ephesians 6:10)

We start together by remembering who our God is. We bring to mind the God that we stand with. This the God whom we proclaim, live for and are in an intimate dynamic relationship with. God is spirit, yet He is also a personal and infinite being (John 4:24). God is one in substance, nature and being, who is incapable of division (Deuteronomy 6:4, 1 Corinthians 8:6).

Yet God is also three persons of equal standing, or the Trinity. It is through reading and studying the Bible, that we discover what gives Him joy and what pleases, angers or offends Him. The words revealed in the Bible describe His attributes. The fact we are able to take hold and understand this about an infinite God is evidence that God desires to be known by humans, including you and me.

What are some of the attributes of our God that we are to be reminded of? There are two different kinds of attributes: natural and moral. Firstly, are what are called the natural attributes of God. God is eternal, that is God is without beginning or end. He is the Alpha and Omega (Revelation 21:6). God is outside of time, time is within God, and He is free from the succession of time. God lives in the eternal present, as past, present and future, are now for God. He is the *'I AM'* or *'YAHWEH'*, which is the personal name of God (Exodus 3:14–15). God is immanent. That is, God is always there. He is very near, everywhere and wholly present everywhere, as He fills the universe in all its parts without division (Psalm 139:7–12; Jeremiah 23:23–24). This is our God.

God is omnipotent. That means God has unlimited power to do all things that are the object of power. With Almighty God nothing is impossible, yet there are things God cannot do such as He cannot do

Section C: Weapon of Memory

anything that is contrary to His own nature. For instance, He cannot declare something infinite if that something is finite. Omnipotence is an essential quality of God for if God were not all–powerful then He would not be God and would not be worthy of worship. God stopped the sun during Joshua's time (Joshua 10:12–15). Amazing power! God created the universe with His eternal and infinite power! God made everything out of nothing, and He sustains it and gives all of it life! What an amazing God! This God, our God, is immutable, in that He is unchangeable:

"I AM the LORD and I do not change." (Malachi 3:6)

"Jesus Christ is the same yesterday, today and forever." (Hebrews 13:8)

God is infinite because He has no limits. God has an internal and a qualitative absence of limitation, with boundless activity (Romans 11:33; 1 Timothy 1:16). God is also life (John 14:6), energy and activity. God has and is, all power and powerful. He has the power to do all things that are the object of power. With God all things are possible (Luke 1:37). For as the prophet Jeremiah clarifies:

"Nothing is too hard for you!" (Jeremiah 32:17)

Additionally, God is omniscient, because He has all knowledge! God has perfect knowledge of all things: actual, past, present, future and possible. God knows all things (1 John 3:20) and has infinite understanding of all things (Psalm 147:5). He knows all that we do, including the remembrance of all that we have done, all that we think and say, and all that we could think and say, as well as a record of those words and thoughts.

[1] You have searched me, Lord, and you know me.
[2] You know when I sit and when I rise;
you perceive my thoughts from afar.

> ³ You discern my going out and my lying down;
> you are familiar with all my ways.
> ⁴ Before a word is on my tongue,
> you, Lord, know it completely. (Psalm 139:1–4)

God is personable, has personality, self–consciousness and is able to communicate freely and openly. God is a free personal Spirit! God is not material, as He is invisible and indestructible (John 4:24; 1 Timothy 1:17; 1 Timothy 6:15–16). He is transcendent, in that God is above and beyond everything in this world and has self–existence apart from and independent of His creation. This reflects God's majesty and greatness (1 Chronicles 29:11; Romans 11:33).

Those are just some of our God's natural attributes. Now we glimpse at His moral attributes, qualities and characteristics. God is goodness personified, because He is absolute perfection, and is always seeking His creation's welfare. The goodness of God has several key parts to these moral attributes. These are grace, because God gives us what we do not deserve. Grace can be defined as God's riches at Christ's expense (Ephesians 2:7). Grace is the unmerited goodness of God (John 1:16), because God is slow to anger and God longs to forgive (Exodus 34:6–7) and God is love (1 John 4:8–10). God communicates and gives of Himself . God is full of mercy, as He does not give humanity what we deserve. The mercy of God is the goodness of God to those who are in distress, and He is filled with tenderness and compassion (Ephesians 2:3–5). God is truth and not only that, because He is also the revelation, source and foundation of all truth, as exemplified by His Son, Jesus Christ who proclaimed concerning Himself :

> "'I am the way and the truth and the life. No one comes to the
> Father except through me." (John 14:6)

Moral excellence and perfection of God is who God is, because God is holiness! That is, He has complete separation from sin. Holiness is who

Section C: Weapon of Memory

and what God is. God declares His holiness (Leviticus 11:44–45; Hebrews 7:26; 1 Peter 1:15) which is seen in action because of, and through, God's absolute righteousness. All of God's actions conform to His holiness. This is our God who can be known personally. As Christians, we are in an intimate relationship with Almighty God.

GOD IS LOVE

> For God so loved the world that He gave His one and only Son, that whoever believes in Him shall not perish but have eternal life. (John 3:16)

> We know and rely on the love God has for us. God is love. Whoever lives in love lives in God, and God in them.
> (1 John 4:16)

This moral excellence of God is founded on His being love. We live in a world that is in love with love. However, what exactly is meant by the word 'love' today, differs greatly depending on who you ask. In the Bible, God's love is revealed which has a rather different nature from our modern ideas about love. The Apostle John does not simply write that God loves, but rather, he clearly states that God is love.

> [7] Dear friends, let us love one another, for love comes from God. Everyone who loves has been born of God and knows God. [8] Whoever does not love does not know God, because God is love. [9] This is how God showed His love among us: He sent His one and only Son into the world that we might live through Him. (1 John 4:7–9)

God is the Holy Trinity, that is three persons in one. The Trinity is a living, vibrant community which is sustained by its interactions. Those interactions are of the best and truest nature of love. Every activity of the Trinity is an expression of love, as that is God's very nature. God's love is seen as unfailing, everlasting, intimate, sacrificial, conquering, immeasurable and all–knowing. How is God's love seen?

Firstly, God's love is seen supremely in that He has given His Son, Jesus Christ, to be the Saviour of the world, so that if a person takes up the opportunity that offers to move them into the sphere of His love, they can know and enjoy God in a personal relationship. God had only one Son, Jesus Christ, and He sent Him on a rescue mission to seek the lost and to reconcile people to God. That is love in action.

Secondly, God's love is shown when we as Christians show love. This is where love means a reflection of the love of God, even if only a pale reflection. As a Christian, we are a child of God, so we are to desire to be like our Heavenly Father. We do this by showing the world around us, through our love for others and our transformed character.

The Christian Church is to be a community of love, for this is how the world sees God and thinks the Church should be. If people see a Christian that is not loving and kind, rightly or wrongly, the whole Church is branded as a bunch of fakes and hypocrites. Worse still, God is seen at best as nothing more than a distant uncaring irrelevant figure. The love between Christians ought to be seen as a visible showing of the love of the invisible God. The character of the Church should always to be reflecting God in all aspects. The ultimate example of showing people God, is for us as Christians, to love all others and also to be love to all others without prejudice or bias. People should be seeing God's love, through our love. For as Jesus said,

> [34] 'A new command I give you: love one another. As I have loved you, so you must love one another. [35] By this everyone will know that you are my disciples, if you love one another.'"
> (John 13:34–35)

This love of God, sent from and empowered by God, releases us from the things that can so easily obstruct and complicate our daily walk with Him. The more we hold onto His love, the more we will desire it and the more it will be revealed in our daily life. Our love in action today, reflects God's love in action on the cross of Jesus Christ. As a Christian, we are to be so filled and magnetized with God's love and grace, that it acts as a compelling attraction to others of the majestic goodness and love of God! The very God, we Christians love, serve, obey and follow. By loving others in this way, the Gospel becomes attractive and undeniable!

God is love. The Father totally loves the Son and the Spirit. The Son totally loves the Father and the Spirit. The Spirit totally loves the Father and the Son. God shows love and commands us to love one another so that He will be seen. When we show love, we are therefore reflecting and revealing God in whose image we are made.

GOD AS KING

Our God is a God who is also sovereign and has authority and sovereignty over all things. The sovereignty of God means that God is in control at all times, and nothing can occur outside of His control and will. He won't deny people their humanity when dealing with them.

As a sovereign God, He issues decrees. Firstly, there are the sovereign decrees of God. This is when God says things such as 'Eternal life is available for all'. We may choose to accept the invitation and be called His child, or we can reject it. It is a choice. As a Christian, we have taken up God's offer and we are trusting and obeying Him for all aspects of life.

Secondly there are God's conditional decrees, where God says, "I am willing to give you our opinion and help when you ask." Our reaction then, should be to hear Him speak as we read the Bible, and talk to God in prayer about the situation.

Thirdly there are the natural decrees, which are shown when God creates a lemon tree. That lemon tree will not produce potatoes. Our reaction to these decrees, should be to plan in view of that kind of thinking. A question often posed, particularly accused by Satan through others, is one that goes "Well if God is sovereign, then why doesn't He do something about the suffering of so many people such as those who are dying for lack of food?" But God has done something about it. God has supplied enough food for all people everywhere. Nevertheless, people are greedy, particularly in the West, and they do not necessarily want to share that food. Subsequently, the problem is not with God, but with people. God's provision to all people has become God's provision for the minority, through humanity's inhumanity to others.

As for other kinds of suffering, that's part of the reason for the cross of Jesus Christ. This is where God Himself experienced human suffering when Jesus, the Son of God, died on the cross. Jesus Christ was the man who was both fully God and fully human. God is not so removed from our sufferings. We know this because He Himself endured and suffered the Cross. Just because God allows free will which gives people the freedom to sin, that doesn't mean that God is responsible for the sin. That is, and must remain, the responsibility of the person who transgressed. If it were not so, we would simply be mindless automatons instead of persons with free will. God's sovereignty is inclusive in that it covers all our actions, whether they are good or bad (Acts 2:23; Ephesians 2:10).

The foundation of God's sovereignty is wisdom according to Paul (Ephesians 3:8–11). Therefore, when we are faced with a decision, God knows what is going to occur and He knows all the options and choices. It is important for us when faced with making decisions to read the Bible, speaking to God about the decisions and waiting to hear Him speak to us. God is interested in every facet of our life. If He were not, then He couldn't be personal, and He certainly wouldn't be sovereign.

We remember that this is our God, and that the victory has been achieved and proclaimed.

Section C: Weapon of Memory

Encouragement From Other Sojourners

God is no stop–gap; he must be recognized at the centre of life, not just when we are at the end of our resources; he wills to be recognized in life, and not just when death comes; in health and vigour, and not just in suffering; in our activities, and not just in sin.[50]

God claims omnipotence for Himself , and wants us to acknowledge it. God's omnipotence is not futile, idle and inactive as some theologians pretend, but caring effective, energetic and always active. It is not an omnipotence which can only serve as a general influence in uncertainty (like ordering a stream to stay inside a prescribed channel), but one which focuses on specific and definite events.[51]

It is not merely others who have found the living God who accompany us; it is the living God Himself. His presence guards, consoles and challenges us, energising us as we journey. The God who is the goal of our travelling is also our companion on the journey.[52]

A lot of people don't understand how I, in the light of so much contradictory evidence, could possibly believe in God. What I don't understand is how he, in the light of even more contradictory evidence, could possibly believe in me.[53]

---

[50] Bonhoeffer, Page 111
[51] Calvin, Page 70–71
[52] McGrath, Page 65
[53] Skinner, Page 96

C3. We Are God's Children

God the Holy Spirit is 'born' into Christians. That is why Jesus said that to be one of His followers, we had to be 'born again' (John 3:3). This phrase can also be translated 'born from above' which emphasises that it is something that we cannot do for ourselves. When we choose to be 'born again' or 'born from above', it is completely through a work of God, and nothing to do with ourselves and our own efforts. That is what happened back in the 1980s, when I became a Christian, a follower and disciple of Jesus Christ. I was 'born again'.

When we are 'born again', it shows that we have bowed the knee before Jesus. It shows that we have said that we want to dedicate our whole life to Him, that we want to live for Him with every fibre of our being and that we want to have the Holy Spirit in our life. What is the result of our being born again? Having accepted the Father's call to be born again, we have been declared a new creation (2 Corinthians 5:17) who is created to be like God in true righteousness and holiness in a lifelong process of regeneration (Ephesians 4:24). We are washed by rebirth and renewal through the Holy Spirit who has come to live within us (Titus 3:5).

As a consequence, we are now truly alive. Not just physically but also now spiritually (Ephesians 2:5). Not because of anything we have done but all because of Jesus Christ and His love of us and for us. Now that we are 'born again', God has accepted us as a member of His family with all the legal standing of an heir and of that as a truly beloved child of His. Isn't that just an amazing fact about the Christian life? Here is how Paul goes on to explain it:

> [4] But when the set time had fully come, God sent His Son, born of a woman, born under the law, [5] to redeem those under the law, that we might receive adoption to sonship. [6] Because you are His sons, God sent the Spirit of His Son into our hearts, the Spirit who calls out, 'Abba, Father.' [7] So you are no longer a

slave, but God's child; and since you are His child, God has made you also an heir. (Galatians 4:4–7)

Because God has adopted us as His very own child, we can know God has bought us from our slavery to sin and self. We realize that He has placed us into a family (Ephesians 1:5–7). His family. We can be assured that God will supply all our needs, just as all good fathers do. God Himself , comes to live inside us through His Spirit (Ephesians 2:22).

This symbolizes that we are now reconciled with God, even though once we were separated from Him and was His enemy (Romans 5:10). Resulting from this, we have transformed relationships with God, with other people and also with our own selves (John 15:9–12). Now as a child of the living God, we are to seek God's honour and glory in all things, rather than our own glory and honour (John 17:10). We have come into the light from the darkness (John 8:12; John 12:46; Ephesians 5:8). We are an adopted and born–again disciple living in the light of Jesus Christ, knowing that He is truly the way, the truth and the life (John 14:6). As Christians, followers of Jesus Christ, we will be undergoing life change as we continue to be transformed increasingly into the image of Jesus Christ. This is where we are learning to be like Jesus in every part of our life, practising living in His presence and engaging our life so intimately with Him that He truly lives through us. With all of that, there comes a change in our goal in life.

> ³ We know that we have come to know him if we keep his commands. ⁴ Whoever says, 'I know him,' but does not do what he commands is a liar, and the truth is not in that person. ⁵ But if anyone obeys his word, love for God is truly made complete in them. This is how we know we are in him: ⁶ whoever claims to live in him must live as Jesus did. (1 John 2:3–6)

The goal of being a Christian, is to walk and live as Jesus did and to follow the commands of Jesus. This means that we, as followers of Jesus

Christ, are to be living a life worthy of that of Jesus. We are to want Him to be our Lord over every aspect of our life here on earth. This means we are to rely totally on Jesus and denying ourselves for all things, which is now to be our goal in our life as a Christian.

This is possible only through totally submitting ourselves to the Holy Spirit in all facets of life and leading a life of constantly dealing with God in all matters. That is how we, as Christians, are to be radical, holy and endeavouring to reach the goal of being Jesus to others. This is done by being constantly renewed in the attitude of our mind (Ephesians 4:23) and having a heart willing to be transformed. It is by loving others in such a way, that the end of our generosity is only when our resources have expired.

The world will know that we are God's person, if we show love towards others, whether they are Christians or not. As Christians, we have a goal to be radical and holy, in a lifelong process of transformation. We are to be obedient to Jesus in loving God and loving others – including those who are our enemies. How can we do and be that? If we try that in our own strength we will fail. It is only through the power, strength and wisdom of the Holy Spirit who lives within us, that we can be capable of doing this.

WE ARE ASSURED

> [1] Everyone who believes that Jesus is the Christ is born of God, and everyone who loves the father loves His child as well. [2] This is how we know that we love the children of God: by loving God and carrying out His commands. [3] In fact, this is love for God: to keep His commands. And His commands are not burdensome, [4] for everyone born of God overcomes the world. This is the victory that has overcome the world, even our faith. [5] Who is it that overcomes the world? Only the one who believes that Jesus is the Son of God. (1 John 5:1–5)

Section C: Weapon of Memory

When we became a Christian, we admitted that we had done wrong against God and His ways. We came to believe and trust in Jesus Christ as King and Lord. We have called on Him, received, trusted, obeyed and worshipped Him, recognized Him for who He is and what He has done; we have confessed Jesus as our Lord and Saviour. Then because of this confession, belief and trust, we are a Christian, and started following Jesus Christ.

However, since that time, there have been times when we doubted whether or not we are God's child. There are times when we don't feel saved, and we still feel condemned and don't feel any certainty that we are a Christian. There are occasions when we don't feel spiritual or sometimes, we question privately whether we have a new life. The archenemy, Satan, loves to tell us such lies. Even the Apostle Paul seems to have some sort of similar experience to this when He was faced with a crisis when in Corinth (1 Corinthians 2).

What is certain, is that emotions and feelings have a part to play in our salvation. When we experience the enjoyment of a quiet inner confidence that only comes from the Spirit, as we became a follower of Jesus – that is feeling and emotion. However, being a Christian is not to be based on our emotional feelings but rather the assured promises of God. Emotional feelings can come and go according to our state of health. God's promises, however, are true, dependable and solid. God the Father has promised us salvation through His Son Jesus in the power of the Holy Spirit.

Jesus, the Son of God, promised us a life of abundance and a foretaste of eternity. His promise was not only for our future glorious home in heaven, but for our present struggle laden home on earth. Where He sits at the right hand of the Father, He continually prays for us. When we became a follower of Jesus, God started living within us through His Spirit, and we are a part of the universal and historical Church of Jesus Christ. This assures us of our faith and belief in a God of mercy and love. A great witness and assurance of our faith is that of our life being transformed. We can look back on our life and see how we have changed. Some things will have changed instantly, and other things will have changed much slower. We will continue to change the more we rely on God to change and transform us into the image of His Son, Jesus Christ. Our salvation does not depend on how much we have of God, but rather, on how much He has of us, and how much control we are allowing the Holy Spirit to have of us. How very beautiful, assuring and encouraging is that to know. We can be assured that we are, indeed, beloved children of the living God.

WE ARE BLESSED

As Christians, we are blessed by God in seven ways because of Jesus Christ. We have peace with God (Romans 5:1) due to God's great mercy, which has declared peace to all those who accept salvation through Jesus' death on the Cross. Isn't that amazing? What is more, we have access to God now. When Jesus died, He tore the veil (Luke 23:45) and broke down the barrier between God and humanity (Ephesians 2:14). As Christians, we have immediate access to God, through our faith in Jesus Christ, and Him alone. No other religion or faith can say that! Going on, it means we have a glorious hope to come. Peace with God takes care of the past, in that He no longer holds our sins against us. Access to God takes care of our present, so that we can come to Him whenever we desire. A glorious hope takes care of our future, when we will one day share in His glory (Romans 5:2).

We go onto develop Christian character (Romans 5:3–4). Being a Christian and justified before God is no escape from the sufferings and trials in this world, but for us as believers, suffering and trials are for our own good (Romans 8:28). We endure for the sake of the Gospel. Suffering develops our patience and perseverance; patience and perseverance grows our character, and through character, we have a glorious hope. We can do this only because we have God's love within us (Romans 5:5–8). The love of God is poured into our heart. We experience the complete and absolute love, peace and joy of God. This inner experience of this love is through the Holy Spirit who sustains us as we go through sufferings and trials. Faith, hope and love all combine to give us the patience to endure the trials of life.

We also have salvation from future wrath (Romans 5:9–10). God will keep on saving us, now that we love Him. We need strength to endure suffering and persecution, remembering that as we stand firm in faith, we will in the end be saved. Saved because we have reconciliation with God (Romans 5:11). We have fellowship with God, because we are reconciled with Him because of Jesus' death on the cross. God in His mercy sent His Son, Jesus as a peacemaker, that we may return to fellowship with Him. We are to rejoice in our present enjoyment of reconciliation with God (Romans 5:1b, 10), and rejoice that all this comes through Jesus Christ, our Master, Lord and Saviour.

Through Jesus Christ, and Him alone, we have these seven blessings of peace, access, hope, transformation, indwelling, love, salvation and reconciliation. These seven blessings show how certain and assured that salvation is in Jesus Christ and through Him alone, for us and for all those who choose it.

WE ARE PARTAKERS

To partake, or to be a partaker of something, can mean at least three things. Firstly, it means to have a share in something by looking for or having the qualities or attributes of that thing. Second: it can mean having, giving or receiving something. Finally, to partake of something, can also mean to consume. Jesus Christ was a partaker, because when He became human, He adorned human flesh and blood

> [14] Since the children have flesh and blood, He too shared in their humanity so that by His death He might break the power of Him who holds the power of death – that is, the devil – [15] and

free those who all their lives were held in slavery by their fear of death. ¹⁶ For surely it is not angels He helps, but Abraham's descendants. ¹⁷ For this reason He had to be made like them, fully human in every way, in order that He might become a merciful and faithful high priest in service to God, and that He might make atonement for the sins of the people. ¹⁸ Because He Himself suffered when He was tempted, He is able to help those who are being tempted. (Hebrews 2:14–18.)

As Christians, we are also partakers, for we are to hunger and thirst for righteousness or in other words, be partakers of righteousness. That adds up the meanings of the definition above, whereby we are to share in, receive and consume righteousness. In this pursuit of partaking after righteousness, the New Testament has a lot to say about what we as Christians are to be partakers of. We are a partaker when we participate in communion, as a partaker and participant at the Lord's Table (1 Corinthians 10:14–21). We are partakers of spiritual things (Romans 15:25–27), the Gospel (1 Corinthians 9:19–23) and of suffering and consolation (2 Corinthians 1:6–7). We are partakers of God's grace (Philippians 1:3–7) and holiness (Hebrews 12:10–11). We are partakers of Jesus Christ's suffering (1 Peter 4:12–13), the glory that will one day be revealed (1 Peter 5:1–4) as well as being partakers of the divine nature through God's promises (2 Peter 1:1–4). These are the things we are to partake of. They help lead us into a full experience of the Christian life, in order to go and tell the gospel of Jesus Christ.

We remember that we are God's child and that we are assured, blessed and a partaker.

Section C: Weapon of Memory

Encouragement From Other Sojourners

You want me to tell you why God is to be loved and how much. I answer, the reason for loving God is God Himself; and the measure of love due to Him is immeasurable love.[54]

God lets himself be pushed out of the world onto the cross. He is weak and powerless in the world, ant this precisely the way, the only way, in which he is with us and helps us. Matthew 8:17 makes it clear that Christ helps us, not by virtue of his omnipotence, but by virtue of his weakness and suffering.[55]

By the word 'repentance', then, I understand new birth. Its sole aim is to form in us the image of God which was spoilt and almost destroyed by Adam's sin.[56]

Let us then 'look unto Jesus', let us follow His example. As the enemy comes and attacks the mind and the understanding, let us answer Him by 'the blessed hope', the certainty of it, the glory of it. And let us realise that we are in His power, and that He will never leave us nor forsake us.[57]

---

[54] Bernard, Page 3
[55] Bonhoeffer, Page 134
[56] Calvin, Page 155–156
[57] Lloyd-Jones01, Page 321

C4. We Converse With God

> [18] And pray in the Spirit on all occasions with all kinds of prayers and requests. With this in mind, be alert and always keep on praying for all the Lord's people. [19] Pray also for me, that whenever I speak, words may be given me so that I will fearlessly make known the mystery of the gospel, [20] for which I am an ambassador in chains. Pray that I may declare it fearlessly, as I should. (Ephesians 6:18–20)

Paul knew the value of prayer and the necessity of it in his life. He knew that prayer is to be at the centre of the Christian's relationship with God. As Christians, we can openly converse with God, with reverence and fear but also with great intimacy and genuineness. Prayer is how we as Christians, are energized to keep persevering for Him. Fighting in our own power is useless. When we talk to God, we are strengthening our relationship with Him. When we ask other Christians to pray for us, Church unity is strengthened. A solo Christian is an anomaly. Except in extreme circumstances, there is always a way to ask others for prayer and help.

Prayer is the major action of fellowship between God and humanity, and of humans communicating with God, both in talking and listening (Genesis 18:33). Prayer is the prime way of "letting God in" to our life as Christians, and of enjoying the company of God, relating all aspects of life to Him. It is reporting back to God of all that is going in our life and what our hopes for the future are. Prayer is also a means of protection for us as Christians, in that often we are too weak in our own understanding and strength to withstand all that is against us. God Himself assists us as we pray, correcting and strengthening our yearnings and please. Prayers expressing our desires and thoughts go on to offer a contributory way to our journey through life. Prayer is ultimately what we humans were made for. That is conversing and

Section C: Weapon of Memory

communicating with God. This dynamic relationship enables us as Christians to engage in prayer that is both personal and relational.

However, prayer is only the penultimate stage in our relationship with God. Prayer is the forerunner of the day when we Christians will know fully, even as we are fully known (1 Corinthians 13:12). All prayer consists of our desires or longings to know God better, and that is to be our prime motivation: to know God better. That is why it is a spiritual weapon, and also why Satan tries to stop Christians from praying, particularly praying with other Christians.

The very function of prayer, the act of communicating and conversing with God, reveals our constant hunger for God's help and consolidates our desire towards the ultimate goal, which is a life of eternal joy, happiness, worship and knowledge of God. It is through the Bible that our desire to know God and be known by God changes and develops. That is why prayer and Bible reading go hand in hand. Prayer emits our words to the God we seek to know increasingly, as a response to His reaching out to us. Through prayer, God is able to comprehend us regardless of language, grammar or oratory skill, as long as we approaches with a correct attitude. Words are not just to be a mental action but also an emotive act, conveying emotions and feeling. Prayer is to convey deep emotions, feelings and expressions to God, regardless of our language skills. The words spoken in our prayers are to portray our innermost feelings and desires to Him.

Because God is personal, He values language and expects us to talk to Him. If for some reason, we are unable to convey words in prayer, then we can know and rest in the knowledge that the Holy Spirit will intercede on our behalf (Romans 8:26). Prayer epitomises the Father–child relationship symbolized in the Christian's relationship with God. It further symbolizes the freedom and peace which we can be found in prayer, advocated by Jesus to communicate His deepest desires. We see this in Jesus' final prayers before He went to the Cross (John 17). We can feel His agony and raw emotion as He starts to pray.

Engaged in Battle

[1] After Jesus said this, he looked towards heaven and prayed: 'Father, the hour has come. Glorify your Son, that your Son may glorify you. [2] For you granted him authority over all people that he might give eternal life to all those you have given him. [3] Now this is eternal life: that they know you, the only true God, and Jesus Christ, whom you have sent. [4] I have brought you glory on earth by finishing the work you gave me to do. [5] And now, Father, glorify me in your presence with the glory I had with you before the world began. (John 17:1–3)

LORD'S PRAYER

[9] 'This, then, is how you should pray:
'"Our Father in heaven, hallowed be your name,
[10] your kingdom come, your will be done,
on earth as it is in heaven.
[11] Give us today our daily bread.
[12] And forgive us our debts,
as we also have forgiven our debtors.
[13] And lead us not into temptation,
but deliver us from the evil one."
(Matthew 6:9–13)

Jesus taught His disciples to pray. In Luke's account, he says that they asked for Jesus to teach them (Luke 11:1). This example is often called the "Lord's Prayer". This is not because Jesus Himself, would have prayed it. He was without sin, so He would have had no need to have said, "forgive us our debts" (Matthew 6:12). This prayer was given by Jesus, as a model for His disciples' prayers to be like. Hence Jesus saying, "This, then, is how you should pray" (Matthew 6:9). This is, in all probability, the prayer that is most frequently used, and repeated, by those professing to be Christians and also by those who are not.

Section C: Weapon of Memory

Father: Calling God, "Father", implies that God is in a personal relationship with us as a disciple, and we can joyfully think of Him as a loving and generous Father. God is not impersonal but wants to be approached intimately as a child approaches its daddy. By saying "our Father", as an individual Christian, we realize that we are not alone, but are part of a wider Church family.

Holy: Hallowed means holy and when we call God 'Hallowed', it is symbolic of our intimate adoration of Him and means that we are to place Him and His purposes at the top of our list. God is to be number one priority in all aspects of our life and of the world. God's glory, kingdom and will are to be our supreme concern, high above our own needs.

Kingdom: God is a King, and He rules. Jesus has inaugurated the Kingdom of God. He is its King. The Kingdom is not yet complete so we Christians must pray that it will become more and more complete. This is where we pray that the Gospel will spread far and wide, and God's Kingdom will grow until the time when Jesus Christ returns in glory, to rule with majesty and honour.

Will: As God is holy and a king, His Will is already being done in heaven. We are to pray that life here on earth will approximate to life in heaven as the Kingdom grows. We are to want to place God as our number one priority and to see God's kingdom spread. We also pray that God's Will shall be our top priority as well. They are the three priorities for the Christian: God will be number one; His Kingdom will spread, and His will be done on earth.

Give: This signifies that as Christian, we need to rely on and trust in God for all things that are necessary for life to continue. As Christians, we are to be thankful, for all the good gifts that Father God has supplied to us, quite often without our needing to ask Him to supply.

Forgiveness: Forgiveness of course is a major part of Christianity, both in the way that God forgives us when we come to Him in penitence and repentance, but also in the way that we forgive others, including ourselves. Asking for forgiveness can be one of the hardest things we can to do. In times like that, it is best that we to stop and consider Jesus Christ and the enormity of His forgiveness. If He can forgive, and does forgive us for all we that have done wrong, then we also should forgive others, regardless of how difficult that might be to do. Forgiveness deals with our emotional response towards those who have transgressed against us. Forgiveness enables us to have the same openness toward the person after they offended us, as before. When we forgive the offender, the hurt and the wound will start to diminish. This is helped when we realise Jesus Christ understands what we are undergoing and that we can use these experiences for our eternal benefit and advantage.

Temptation: Temptations are an undeniable and inevitable fact of the Christian's life. But it is good to know that temptations are common experiences for all Christians, and not just for us as individuals, no matter what we may think at the time. Temptation itself is not sin. Rather it is the giving into temptation that causes us to sin. It is not just out and out temptation that Jesus means but the tests and trials of life as well. We can overcome both temptations and trials, in order that our character, through the power of the indwelling Holy Spirit, will become more like that of Jesus Christ, the Master.

Deliver: What we are delivered from, is better translated as "evil one" rather than "evil". Satan is the one who tempts us. It is He who suggests to us that we should not forgive others and to trust in ourselves for our own needs. It is He who does not want God to be number one or for God's will to be done on earth as in heaven. It is Satan who does not want God's kingdom to be spread. Neither does He want Jesus Christ to return in glory. Therefore, as Christians, we are to pray for these things to happen and to happen quickly. We need to rely and trust in God for deliverance from Satan, who wants to snatch away our inner joy and our total dependence on God.

Section C: Weapon of Memory

Your power: God deliver us from temptation, trials and Satan, because He is always all–powerful and eternally almighty. As Christians, we are to rely on God's strength to overcome temptations, trials and Satan. We are not to do as we often do, which is to rely on our own strength. By relying on our own strength, failure is inevitable, but by trusting in God and His power and strength, then assuredly we can overcome temptation, trials and Satan.

Your glory: This is our aim as Christians, whereby we are to give all glory to God, regardless of what personal achievements have been gained. His glory is to be our supreme concern, so that God is number one in our life as Christians. Consequently, we pray that God's will is done in us and in the world, so that His kingdom does indeed continue to grow until Jesus Christ returns in majesty and glory.

We can pray, converse with God, at any time and in any place. Silently, out loud and with a full expression of our being, knowing that God loves us, loves to hear our voice as we approach Him in reverence, humility and love. God loves to hear our praises of adoration, confession of our sins, thanksgiving for all that He has done and the of placing our requests and needs before Him.

Here is a question we have all asked at one time or another. Does God answer all our prayers? Yes, He most certainly does! Although the answer we expect, may not be the answer we get. So often we pray, expecting one result and getting another and then think that God hasn't answered our prayer. Sometimes the answer He gives is 'yes'. At other times it may be 'no' or 'not yet'. When we come to realise that God works outside of our restrictions of time and space, we continue to learn to trust His judgement and wisdom. We acknowledge that He is the Master, and we are but one of His servants.

Alas, sometimes during prayer, our attitude is that we are the master, and God is our servant. There could be any number of reasons, as to why some prayers remain unanswered. It could possibly be that the prayers that aren't answered may be due to our having in our life things such as unconfessed sin (Psalm 66:18), doubt (James 1:5–7), selfishness (James 4:3), disobedience (Proverbs 28:9) or pride (Luke 18:9–14). Or it could just be for no reason that we can possibly see or understand during this life here on earth.

We remember that prayer is a weapon for spiritual warfare.

Section C: Weapon of Memory

Encouragement From Other Sojourners

The flesh will murmur against you, but it will be bridled by fervour of spirit. The old serpent will sting and trouble you, but prayer will put him to flight and by steadfast, useful toil the way will be closed to him.[58]

Prayer enables us to explore the riches which are treasured up for us with our heavenly Father. There is real contact between God and men when they enter the upper sanctuary, appear before Him and claim His promises. … Prayer digs up the treasures which the Gospel reveals to the eye of faith. The need for prayer, and its usefulness, cannot be emphasised too much.[59]

Prayer is a strong wall and fortress of the church; it is a Godly Christian's weapon, found only by those who have the spirit of grace and of prayer.[60]

Is there a place for comedy in prayer? If there's a place for comedy in life, there's a place for comedy in prayer. God is a tough audience as far as audible response is concerned, but I love that I don't have to explain the references.[61]

We should enjoy our freedom in prayer as a true son or daughter of our heavenly father. We can be natural, bold and joyfully confident as we pray.[62]

---

[58] à Kempis, Page 80
[59] Calvin, Page 204
[60] Luther, Page 212
[61] Skinner, Page 4
[62] Watson, Page 120

C5. We Keep On Learning About God

> "For the time will come when people will not put up with sound doctrine. Instead, to suit their own desires, they will gather around them a great number of teachers to say what their itching ears want to hear." (2 Timothy 4:3)

Are these words not indicative of where some parts of the Church, particularly in the west, are today? There are Churches and ministries where preachers and teachers prefer to tickle the ears of their listeners, instead of stirring people into transformed lives for Jesus Christ.

STUDY

The words which are translated as "doctrine" are found frequently in the letters written by Paul, chiefly in the Pastoral Epistles of 1 & 2 Timothy and Titus. Doctrine is the study of God and the ways and purposes of God, as revealed through the pages of the Bible. The more we as Christians learn about God and put that learning into practise in our daily life, the more we will be able to deal with the daily pressures of living in our communities which are ever distancing and alienating themselves from God.

Moreover, we will continue learning and understanding the very nature of God whom we serve. Availing ourselves of His strength, we will be able to both act and react rightly in varying circumstances. In doing these things, we will continue to develop our relationship with God and serve Him. Doctrine is for all Christians regardless of their status in the Church they attend. Doctrine is for all those who are Christians, whether they are a Church leader or an ordinary Church member who sits in the congregation. Doctrine is for us as Christians, regardless of our level of academic achievement and regardless of the length of time we have been a Christian.

Section C: Weapon of Memory

Doctrine matters for us as Christians, because ultimately, what we believe about God, affects how we will behave. If we have good, solid, biblical doctrine being practised in our life, we will show that we are seeking to live a righteous life of complete and total obedience to Jesus Christ who is our Lord and Master.

How so? For we are to hunger and thirst after righteousness (Matthew 5:6) and this can only come about through the work of the indwelling Holy Spirit. Our mind is renewed and transformed (Romans 12:1) with the teachings of and about Jesus Christ. This is done as we practice what our mind learns and therefore our whole life is transformed to the glory of God. It is when that has happened, that people ask us regarding the reason as to why we have been transformed. We are asked questions regarding the reason for the hope that we as Christians grasp onto. It is in this way the Gospel and Good News of Jesus Christ is spread. That is one of the ultimate reasons why doctrine is important. It is also evangelism.

The need to learn and practice true biblical doctrine is ultimately important when faced with persecution for being a Christian. If our faith were to be based on anything less than the belief in Jesus Christ as both God and man, then ultimately that foundation will break, and there can be no hope for us. If as Christians, we are only seeking to have our ears tickled with what we want to hear, then enduring persecution for being a Christian, would be much harder than if we had had a solid doctrinal teaching about living the Christian life. With solid doctrinal teaching, as Christians, we have an unending hope, which the Spirit would use to enable us to endure and persevere through any persecution.

Another reason, learning solid doctrine is important is so that we will be able to discern the difference between true apostolic and biblical teaching from the false teachings espoused by false teachers, cults and from those who want to lead us astray. Satan uses these people and movements to lead Christians away from the truth of Jesus Christ.

As Paul writes to Titus:

> "He must hold firmly to the trustworthy message as it has been taught, so that He can encourage others by sound doctrine and refute those who oppose it." (Titus 1:9)

Or again, as Paul writes to Timothy:

> "As I urged I when I went into Macedonia, stay there in Ephesus so that I may command certain men not to teach false doctrines any longer." (1 Timothy 1:3)

> "If anyone teaches false doctrines and does not agree to the sound instruction of my Lord Jesus Christ and to godly teaching, He is conceited and understands nothing."
> (1 Timothy 6:3–4)

Our following Jesus Christ is to be fulltime, 24 hours of the day, every day, as we partake of righteousness as commanded by Jesus Christ. We can engage in active daily discipleship, through learning true biblical doctrine. By continuing to learn biblical doctrine, we will be enabled to discern those true beliefs from false beliefs proposed by others and ultimately engage that biblical doctrine into living a life worthy of Jesus and all for His praise and glory.

READ AND MEDITATE

The Psalmist describes the benefits of reading and meditating upon the Bible (Psalm 119). God's words become a delight to the Psalmist as He follows God's decrees. He gets a sense of wonder which is instilled as God's word is meditated upon. Strength overcomes tiredness as the Psalmist listens to God speaking through the Bible.

For some people and religions, meditation is passive and involves being quiet, saying a chant, letting the mind go blank and seeking to

Section C: Weapon of Memory

experience God. However, meditation for us as Christians is to be active. It is the filling of our mind with the Bible and not the emptying of thought. It is also not seeking to experience God's presence, as God is always present with the Christian through the indwelling of the Holy Spirit. Meditation is where our imagination is involved and allows God to speak through the Bible.

How is this done? Whilst aiming at the positive and the renewing of our mind, mental prayer is a meditation, which involves both our reason and intellect. The use of reason and intellect in meditation is achieved through the mental and spiritual process of reading the Bible, so that it becomes a living part of the Christian's life. By internalising God's words from the Bible into our heart and mind, God's thoughts become our thoughts. Meditating on the Bible enables the words of the Bible to infiltrate all areas in our life. For meditation to be effective, silence and solitude are prerequisites. However, silence and solitude should not mean loneliness but rather be an aid to meditation, reflection, understanding and peace.

One example of how to mediate involves memorization, visualization, personalization and activation. Memorization is to rebuild our thought patterns by memorising words in the Bible passages especially those related to problems we may be facing or those that glorify God. Visualization is to try and understand God's words and thoughts from His point of view. Personalization is to stabilize the emotions expressing the words of Bible in the first person.

Finally, activation, which is to draw new conclusions and make new life–changing decisions based on the Bible. This all helps in the process of becoming more like Jesus in our Christian journey. It also equips us in our battles with Satan and resisting temptations to sins which confront us. Jesus fended off and attacked Satan by using Scripture correctly so as to negate the temptations (Luke 4:1–13). That is why it is a weapon in the spiritual battle. Satan will do all he can to get us to compromise our faith and fall into sin.

Equipped

Reading and meditating on the Bible does many things for us. It equips us for service of God and also to convict us of sin. Then, as it equips, it is essential for evangelism and pointing others to Jesus. The Bible also equips us to give counsel and help to others. Paul urged Timothy to use Scripture when teaching others (2 Timothy 3:16–17).

The Bible is used by the Holy Spirit to equip us to use our spiritual gifts, so that the whole Church, local, national and global, is encouraged, and where God is glorified and honoured. Spiritual maturity derives from building Bible knowledge into our life as a Christian. One of the very key teachings from the Bible is that God can be known personally. Personal knowledge of God is ultimately crucial because knowing God personally and developing the relationship is what being a Christian is all about.

We rejoice that God earnestly desires us to attain this knowledge of Him, in order to increasingly know Him, becoming more like Jesus, developing an intimate knowledge of God and building an active intimacy with Him. The Bible reveals that God has a program for the universe and it is only revealed in the Bible. Therefore, reading and meditation upon the Bible is vital in the life of a Christian. Meditating on the Bible helps us to grow into spiritual maturity and into the ultimate goal of becoming like Jesus. We read and meditate upon the Bible regularly, knowing that the desire to be like Jesus is the goal.

We remember to continue learning from reading and meditating on God's Word, the Bible.

Section C: Weapon of Memory

Encouragement From Other Sojourners

They who are still new and inexperienced in the way of the Lord may easily be deceived and overthrown unless they guide themselves by the advice of discreet persons. ... Yet a little knowledge humbly and meekly pursued is better than great treasures of learning sought in vain complacency. It is better for you to have little than to have much which may become the source of pride.[63]

Meditation was about letting the biblical text impact upon me 'enkindling the emotions' – what a wonderful phrase! – and 'enlightening the understanding. And my heart, as well as my mind, was involved. The worlds of understanding and emotion were brought together, opening the door to a far more authentic and satisfying way of living out the Christian life.[64]

Look, I sound like I'm nagging, but if the priest is going to read these stories to us, week in, week out, you can hardly blame me for remembering and referring to them. I think that was the intention: take away these stories and apply them to your everyday life, employ them in your everyday conversations.[65]

God speaks to us, not primarily to impart information, but to guide our feet, to re–direct our lives, to change us continually into the likeness of Christ. ... We must let God's word address us, challenge us, transform us.[66]

---

[63] à Kempis, Page 72
[64] McGrath, Page 14–15
[65] Skinner, Page 104
[66] Watson, Page 64

C6. We Live Out Joy

[1] Shout for joy to God, all the earth!
[2] Sing the glory of His name; make His praise glorious.
[3] Say to God, 'How awesome are your deeds!
So great is your power that your enemies cringe before you.
[4] All the earth bows down to you;
they sing praise to you,
they sing the praises of your name.'
(Psalm 66:1–4)

There is a life of overwhelming joy that exists between Almighty God and His followers. We get this impression from the sense of a deep intimacy that there is between God and the Psalmist. Part of that intimacy and that relationship was joy, true joy. We can sense where joy fitted into the life of the Psalmist, King David.

Throughout the history of Israel, the majority of scribes and leaders of Israel usually gave praise to God in silence, in meditation and solemnity. This was of course acceptable to God and proper to do so. The Psalmist, among a great number of people, the whole earth is encouraged to shout with exuberant joy to God. It is quite natural for great crowds of people to shout in harmony.

If praise is to be widespread, it must be vocal; joyful sounds stir the soul and cause great thanksgiving to spread throughout the throng of people. Of course, everybody is different, and each person praises differently. There are people who are naturally loud and yet others who are naturally quiet.

Whatever our own style of praise, God is to be praised in all styles and with both the voice and the heart. The whole earth, everything, and everyone, is encouraged by the Psalmist to sing of the glory and power of God. The Psalmist encourages worshippers to turn their praises of joy to God alone. Turning in joy and admiration to a God who one day

Section C: Weapon of Memory

will cause all the earth to fear and tremble before Him. For those who are enemies of God, who have never believed in Him, they too will be forced into giving worship to Him before leaving His presence forever. They will be forced to worship Him, due to His joyful magnificence and through forced submission, not because they choose to. But their worship will not be like those who decided to follow Jesus Christ during their earthly life. The worship of all those who truly believe in Him, following Him intimately, will be of truth, love, service and pure unadulterated joy. Their reward will be to praise God eternally as is due His name alone.

JOY AND THE NATION OF ISRAEL

The Psalmist exhorts great communal joy because of what God has done for Israel (Psalm 66:5–12). He has done mighty works for His people. Did not God start the nation of Israel? Had not God called out the nation of Israel, watching over them, making covenants with Abraham and Moses, promising that He would be their God and they would be His people. The Psalmist exhorts that the nation of Israel were to be a people of joy since they could look and see what God had done for them in the past and, knowing that His ways did not change, they had a sure hope of what He would do for them in the future. They were His and He was theirs. This was cause for great joy.

The Psalmist continues to encourage the people to exhibit joyfulness. God kept the feet of Israel from slipping. Even though Israel often turned their back on Him, God always kept a remnant of true believers for Himself . God sent Israel into exile under stifling enemies, as punishment for their rebellious ways. Eventually He led them into the Promised Land, flowing with milk and honey. That is why Israel could have exultant joy because of the hope they had in their God and the testimony they could give as a nation under their God. Picture this scene of overwhelming joy:

"²³ Moses and Aaron then went into the tent of meeting. When they came out, they blessed the people; and the glory of the LORD appeared to all the people. ²⁴ Fire came out from the presence of the LORD and consumed the burnt offering and the fat portions on the altar. And when all the people saw it, they shouted for joy and fell face down." (Leviticus 9:23–24)

JOY AND THE PSALMIST

Now after rejoicing about the joy of the community, the Psalmist turns to Himself and gets personal. His own joy starts with a sacrifice of vows and burnt offerings – a sacrifice, which costs Him something. The Psalmist has given promises to God and He wants to fulfil those promises. Because of His great joy, the Psalmist tells others of the source of His joy. The Psalmist gives testimony to the love of God, about how He confessed His sins to God, and how God had listened to Him and heard His prayers. The Psalmist shouts out "Listen to what God has done for me!" The people had all seen God's work, but they also needed to hear that He was a gracious God who was full of mercy. The Psalmist has developed an intimate relationship with Almighty God, which is revealed in the joy of the Psalmist through sacrifice, testimony and praise.

What exactly is joy? Is joy merely a form of bloated happiness? Joy is not merely going around everywhere and at all times with a silly grin on your face. That kind of joy is dependent upon circumstances and feelings. The type of joy the Psalmist signs of, was to a certain degree dependent upon circumstances and feelings but He was also talking about that deeper, inner joy that is not so dependent upon such things. The source, object and target of the Psalmist's joy, was God and God alone. This kind of joy, however, is not to be confused with mere pleasure or feeling good. This joy was to be a way of life which permeates every facet of life and not just at an emotional level.

Section C: Weapon of Memory

As Christians, we are instruments in the Church, which is the orchestra of God's joy. Any happiness or pleasure we feel is dependent on our circumstances, whereas true internal and biblical joy is always separated from our circumstances and is a heartfelt response that endures, regardless of the circumstances that we find ourselves in. The world says happiness is looking out for our own interests and negotiating our own personal good in all we do and at all times. The world says the greatest good is our own personal happiness. They also mistakenly call this joy.

But that is not true joy. That kind of happiness or false joy never lasts very long, so the perpetual search for joy and happiness continues in a circle. Just as a dog chases its own tail. Now, in and of itself, happiness is not a bad thing, but in comparison to true joy, well there really is no comparison. True joy results from our praising God, giving testimony of God's glory and of our making sacrifices. Joy is more to do with peace and salvation rather than just a purely emotional state.

Over and over again in the Bible, joy is mentioned alongside peace and salvation. Joy is always for the good of others, not for our own selfish gain. When we give away our will, for the sake of others, we receive the joy that Jesus desired for us. Happiness and joy are radically different. True joy is never to be an end in itself. It is only as we make Jesus Christ our overwhelming first priority, that true joy, almost without our knowing it, comes.

As Christians, the source, object and target of our joy, is to be Jesus Christ and Him alone. Where Jesus is glorified in the power of the Holy Spirit, so is God the Father and this pure, unadulterated joy is released upon us and within us. If we seek joy for joy's sake alone, we will mislay it. Why? Because it cannot actually be caught. We are not to seek mere happiness for happiness sake, which is an anaemic form of joy. This is the message of the happiness industry and it is big business. However, true and unbridled joy is given only by Jesus Christ and we receive it by serving Him and Him alone.

JOY AND SUFFERING

Of course, there are all sorts of barriers to the Christian having and exhibiting true joy. One of the things that will often hamper our living a life of joy is that of suffering. We are not that naïve and to say otherwise would be to deny human experience. Every person who has ever lived, has suffered in some way, particularly including Jesus Christ. In the New Testament, joy is often associated with all kinds of suffering.

One day soon though, we will have a perfect body and full health. One day there will be no more persecution, terrorism, missiles, guns, wars or bombs. No more will humanity's inhumanity to humanity be allowed. No more pain. No more sickness. No more death. No more suffering. No more sin. No more evil of any kind. Suffering of any kind leaves some sort of scar or mark. Physical, emotional or mental scars due to suffering. Scars arise as a result of human life and experiences. Much like a house that has been lived in. Scratches visible in the paintwork. Windows, which are broken or cracked. Human bodies are the same. Our bodies have scars as well. Physical, emotional and mental scars.

Yet, one glorious day those things will be gone. Vanished. Perfection will be attained with exultant joy the result. All this will be to the glory of God and His majestic doing that, that this will occur for us, as we are His beloved child. He lavishes His love upon every facet of our life. Salvation is to be our joy. What does this relationship of joy entail for me?

JOY OVERFLOWING

The Psalmist's intimate relationship with God and his life of joy involved sacrifice, testimony and praise. This is also to be the key to our own joy. During His earthly ministry, Jesus prayed to God the Father, that His apostles would indeed have joy:

Section C: Weapon of Memory

"'I am coming to you now, but I say these things while I am still in the world, so that they may have the full measure of my joy within them." (John 17:13)

Amazingly this was not only for His apostles at the time, but also for all those of all time, who profess to follow Him. Including our own self. As we look around in our daily life, as we go about our daily business, we see faces and eyes devoid of joy. When we look into their eyes, we see a hunger and thirst for joy and imagine how they have searched in their journey of life for true joy. Whether that is through materialism, drugs, sex, alcohol, the search for true joy continues. Sadly, that also includes people who would profess to be Christian.

If we are honest, sometimes we don't feel as if joy is part of us. We look around at the world we live in and see all the misery and injustice; we see human life being wasted by cancer and other diseases, and we don't feel very joyful. But when we do that, we are confusing happiness and true joy. If we have lost the joy of our Christian life, we need to put back into perspective just what God is calling us to do, remember what He has done for us, and look ahead to the promises He has made us. We are to consider if Jesus Christ is still truly first in our lives. As Christians, we can never truly lose joy, but we can mislay it as our priorities get confused and jumbled up.

Once we make a conscious decision to claim the joy hidden in the midst of all kinds of suffering, life becomes a celebration. Joy never denies the sadness, but transforms it into a fertile soil for yet further joy. Joy unbounded if you like. Joy is a relationship because it is Jesus Over Yourself. True joy is the result of being in an intimate relationship with Jesus Christ. Joy stems from our seeking to obey God in all things and through all facets of our life. The joy of Jesus Christ is transferred to us as we enter into a personal relationship with Him and go about the task of serving Him in this world. Joy is to be a quality about us, just as it was a quality of the Lord Jesus Christ. We are His disciple, His follower, and we are to practice joy. Salvation is our joy, and our joy is also to be our salvation as it dances in action. Joy was sacrifice, testimony and praise in the life of Jesus Christ and therefore it is to be for us as well because we are one of His followers.

Firstly, there is praise. Praising God lifts our heart, soul and spirit when we are feeling down. Praising God quietly is also fine, just as praising God loudly, is also fine. We are also not to decry another person's way of praising God but we can choose to be joyful simply that God is being praised. Praising God is not simply to be our going through the motions, because praising God is to be a sacrifice. We are to engage in praising God with effort and not complacency. Praising God the Father joyfully through Jesus Christ the Son, regardless of our feelings, emotions, situations and circumstances, in the power of the Holy Spirit who indwells us. This is part of our being in an intimate and dynamic relationship with God, as this can only be done through the comforting and encouraging power of the Holy Spirit. Praise is a reflection of the inner joy of both the individual Christian and of the community of Christian believers.

Secondly there are the testimonies we can share. Our testimonies which tell people of what Almighty God has done in our life, should cause great joy in both others and ourselves. Hearing people talk about what God has done for them should cause us to have great joy and praising God. Telling others of God's mercy, grace and love towards us is also to be part of our joy. The joy of God bubbling inside of us and demanding that we praise God the Father, through God the Son in the power of God the Holy Spirit. Joy is praise in action. Joy also comes from encouraging others and urging others on to grow in faith. We go together as the Church, God's Orchestra of Joy, into the world, telling others the story of joy and how they can have the joy of salvation through Jesus Christ.

We live out joy.

Section C: Weapon of Memory

Encouragement From Other Sojourners

The true objects of enjoyment, then, are the Father and the Son and the Holy Spirit, who are at the same time the Trinity, one Being, supreme above all, and common to all who enjoy Him, if He is an object, and not rather the cause of all objects, or indeed even if He is the cause of all. For it is not easy to find a name that will suitably express so great excellence, unless it is better to speak in this way: The Trinity, one God, of whom are all things, through whom are all things, in whom are all things.[67]

Absolute seriousness is never without a dash of humour.[68]

"I call it Joy, which is here a technical term and must be sharply distinguished both from Happiness and from Pleasure. Joy (in my sense) has indeed one characteristic, and one only, in common with them; the fact that anyone who has experienced it will want it again. Apart from that, and considered only in its quality, it might almost equally well be called a particular kind of unhappiness or grief. But then it is a kind we want. I doubt whether anyone who has tasted it would ever, if both were in His power, exchange it for all the pleasures in the world. But then Joy is never in our power and pleasure often is."[69]

---

[67] Augustine, Page 16
[68] Bonhoeffer, Page 141
[69] Lewis02, Page 20

C7. We Persevere and Overcome

Do you sometimes you feel just like giving up, throwing it all away and just be buried by whatever is burdening you? Almost every Christians has probably felt like that at one time or another. Particularly when undergoing physical, emotional, mental or spiritual troubles or sufferings.

Whatever it is that confronts us as a Christian, a child of the living God, we are to remember that we are to persevere and consequently overcome. Why? Chiefly because we are not alone in our troubles. We have the powerful presence of the Holy Spirit, the Holy Comforter, living within us. It is He who has seals us as God's children. We persevere with Jesus and overcome. What are the two main things which have endeavoured to derail our faith in Jesus, which corrupt our Christian life, that we have had to face in order to overcome?

WHEN DOUBT SETS IN

Firstly, there are the inevitable doubts which confront us. Success in the Christian life is not an accident, but rather it is a direct result of our living in harmony with the basic principles of life set forth in the Bible. Our Christian life was never a matter of expecting our spiritual maturity to occur overnight. The Bible lays down standards and principles of living which we need to follow with God's strength, if we are to continue living at peace with God, other people, and ourselves. We need to know what God expects of us and what guidelines He has given us to achieve this quality of life. As we apply the principles and guidelines of the Bible to our life, we are being transformed into the likeness of Christ (Romans 8:28–29; 2 Corinthians 3:18).

Jesus said, "I have come to bring them life in all its fullness" (John 10:10). Life in all its fullness is achieved in our life as we allow Jesus Christ to live His life through us, so that we do indeed start to think and

Section C: Weapon of Memory

respond like He would do to people and circumstances. We need to learn how to see circumstances and people from God's perspective, rather than reacting on the basis of feelings. When we respond to circumstances on the basis of our feelings that is when conflict, stress, tension and depression enter. When we respond to circumstances by looking from God's perspective, it builds and shows a transformed character as we become more like Jesus. Indeed, it is a rare person who has not suffered some form of doubt, and asked questions similar to these of Jeremiah:

> [19] You, LORD, reign for ever;
> your throne endures from generation to generation.
> [20] Why do you always forget us?
> Why do you forsake us so long?
> [21] Restore us to yourself, LORD, that we may return;
> renew our days as of old
> [22] unless you have utterly rejected us
> and are angry with us beyond measure.
> (Lamentations 5:19–22)

By doubt, we do not mean as in doubting God's very existence, but rather doubting some aspect of the Christian life such as assurance of salvation or any of the other of God's promises. We also can be found to be doubting a specific attribute of God such as His amazing love for us, His innate sovereignty or infinite goodness. When doubt rises within us concerning God's assured promise of salvation of us, that usually occurs after we have engaged in wilful sin or having lost some form of spiritual battle.

Satan loves to cause us to overthink things and mislead us, casting doubt on such things as our assurance of salvation or of being God's very beloved child. Doubting God's sovereignty can occur after we have experienced a great personal tragedy or after hearing of an international disaster. When this occurs, it is important for us to have faith in God through our knowledge of the Bible and trust in its authority as God's Word. When we do sin and transgress, not only do we forget who we are as God's child, but we also doubt what God has said is true in the Bible. We have to learn to believe and trust God regardless of circumstances however divergent the experience is or was. The originator of a lot of doubt in our life as a Christian is Satan who seeks to devour our testimony about Jesus Christ and His transforming power.

Another source of our doubt is the world we live in, with its own moral codes and perceived wisdom which are contrary to that of God expressed in the Bible. Whereas we gain wisdom from God through having the indwelling Holy Spirit and our reading of the Bible, the views of those around us who are not Christian, often have perceived wisdom that is contrary to the view from the Bible. One only has to look at the perceived wisdom of atheistic scientific materialism countering the Christian arguments.

One final source of doubt is any lingering spiritual immaturity within us. Our doubting whether prayer works or not, is often down to our being double minded (James 1:8). Elsewhere Paul writes that doubt arises because of not knowing the basic doctrines of God (Ephesians 4:14). This source of doubt is only defeated through experience, having a maturing, disciplined life of obedience through prayer, studying the Bible and allowing the Holy Spirit to transform. In doing these things, the relationship between God and the Christian is nurtured and growing.

With all that said, apart from being energized by reading the Bible and praying to God, what are some of the ways in which we can overcome the doubts that often intrude upon us and our Christian life? We can openly and freely confess any doubt to God, and He will listen and cleanse us. If doubts persist, we have people that we can talk to whom we trust and confess to them our doubts. They inevitably help us work things out (James 5:16). We are to exhibit faith and show total trust in God for all aspects of our life. The faith in Him that we have, is a defensive weapon against the mistruths, disinformation and doubts which enter our mind. By maintaining our trust in God's promises and God's power, doubts are extinguished. Another step to overcoming these nagging doubts is to live a life where God alone is honoured and glorified. We are to live the righteousness of Jesus, which has been given to us, which helps overcome any lingering and nagging doubts.

WHEN SUFFERINGS AND TROUBLES CONFRONT

> [16] Therefore we do not lose heart. Though outwardly we are wasting away, yet inwardly we are being renewed day by day. [17] For our light and momentary troubles are achieving for us an eternal glory that far outweighs them all. [18] So we fix our eyes not on what is seen, but on what is unseen, since what is seen is temporary, but what is unseen is eternal.
> (2 Corinthians 4:16–18)

We persevere through sufferings. Naturally, as humans, we either treat sufferings too flippantly or far too seriously. The response that God wants us to have is to be exercised by them. When we undergo any suffering or trouble, we are to commit it to God, endure it and understand that He is faithful and that it will eventuate in His glory and honour and for our own good (Romans 8:28; 1 Peter 4:16).

We are to be joyful when enduring suffering (James 1:2–4). Now that that can be pretty hard to do. However, we are not left alone to our own devices. We remember that the Holy Spirit indwells us as a follower of Jesus. As one of His names suggests, the Holy Comforter, He provides comfort and consolation to us during the difficult times. Just as He perseveres, so are we to do so. His perseverance with us, is in relation to God and His work upon us, with us and within us. This is a direct result of the continuous operation of the Holy Spirit in our life as Christian believers. It is a work of divine grace that is begun in our heart, which is continued and being brought through to completion. As Christians, we will never perish. We have eternal life and we will not be condemned because we have crossed over from death to life (John 5:24). God's whole purpose for us is to transform us into the image of Jesus Christ. His purpose for us is to make us holy. This is again where perseverance for us as Christians comes in. Jesus may well use some form of temporal suffering in order to achieve it, but in the light of eternity, it will not be for long.

> [1] Therefore, since we are surrounded by such a great cloud of witnesses, let us throw off everything that hinders and the sin that so easily entangles. And let us run with perseverance the race marked out for us, [2] fixing our eyes on Jesus, the pioneer and perfecter of faith. For the joy that was set before Him He endured the cross, scorning its shame, and sat down at the right hand of the throne of God. [3] Consider Him who endured such opposition from sinners, so that you will not grow weary and lose heart. (Hebrews 12:1–3)

It was an encouragement for those believers then, as for now today for us, to keep our eyes focussed on Jesus Christ, and be willing to obey Him in all circumstances. We are to run the race with eyes fixed ahead on Him alone, forgetting what is past and not looking back at what in the past had entangled us. Paul encourages us in these words of wisdom and testimony:

> [12] Not that I have already obtained all this, or have already arrived at my goal, but I press on to take hold of that for which Christ Jesus took hold of me. [13] Brothers and sisters, I do not consider myself yet to have taken hold of it. But one thing I do: forgetting what is behind and straining towards what is ahead, [14] I press on towards the goal to win the prize for which God has called me heavenwards in Christ Jesus. (Philippians 3:12–14)

Section C: Weapon of Memory

Yes, it can be hard to forget the things that have gone wrong or been particularly difficult. However, with the help of the Holy Spirit, it is possible. As Christians, we persevere in our relationship with God and show that by being obedient to Him and following Him. We are to ask questions humbly of Him and expect Him to answer, particularly if we don't understand something. We persevere in our prayer life, our relationships with God and with other people. God will persevere with us, turning us gradually transforming us into the image of His Son, Jesus Christ. God will not abandon us, even though we are free to abandon Him. If we did abandon Him, He would still continue to call us back to Himself. As a result, if He perseveres with us, so must we continue to persevere. That is love. His love for us and our love for Him in response.

Character develops and results from our perseverance. As Christians, we are to engage and develop our spiritual maturity, working on improving our works of service and being transformed in the image of Jesus Christ. That is God's ultimate purpose for us. But in order to do that, we need to find out what needs to be developed. These characteristics help us to measure how much the Holy Spirit has been free to develop our character. Character involves our having a balanced private life, keeping in balance our involvement with others and our isolation away from others. We cannot do all we should for others if we are constantly in the company of others. We also need time alone but not as a complete hermit. Our capacity to believe God expands. We regularly ask ourselves, "What is there in our life that we are trusting in God for, that He alone can do?"

In our life, Jesus is to have the complete and utter supremacy as well as honour and glory over all facets of our life, reflecting that we are indeed being transformed into His image.

> [7] But we have this treasure in jars of clay to show that this all-surpassing power is from God and not from us. [8] We are hard pressed on every side, but not crushed; perplexed, but not in

Engaged in Battle

despair; ⁹ persecuted, but not abandoned; struck down, but not destroyed." (2 Corinthians 4:7–9)

For us as Christians, self–confidence is to be Christ–confidence. That isn't egotism. We say to ourselves "I can't lose. We can only make mistakes." Confidence is often spawned, in the right context, by the ability to say no.

> ¹² I know what it is to be in need, and I know what it is to have plenty. I have learned the secret of being content in any and every situation, whether well fed or hungry, whether living in plenty or in want. ¹³ I can do all this through Him who gives me strength. (Philippians 4:12–13)

We are to be a consistent good example to all those who we encounter. Whether we like it or not, people are following and watching us, but are we following Jesus Christ closely? Those who are following and watching us do not do what we tell them to do, but rather do what we do. Persistence & endurance is developing staying power, and our being able to hold courageously to the right course even under extreme difficulties. Things such as unwarranted criticism, difficult circumstances, open opposition and difficult and unwanted problems can stop us cold. If we allow them to. The problem is that we sometimes think that the Christian life is a sprint race, when in fact we have forgotten that it is a marathon, where a second wind of the long hard grind is often necessary.

We often go blazing away from the start line determined to solve all the world's problems this very day. We discover quickly, that doing it this way, we soon run out of energy because we were trying to do it all in our own strength. When that happens, it is often because we refuse to wait for the Holy Spirit to do His steady and sure work in our life. We have had to learn to allow the Holy Spirit top truly be in control of our life. Therefore, we maintain a positive attitude. A danger in

Section C: Weapon of Memory

becoming negative, is that a root of bitterness sets up. The greatest therapy is that of thanksgiving and prayer. God says we can do it. Satan says we can't do it. Who will you listen to?

Then there is resistance. However, this is not resistance to ideas but rather resistance to opposition. Criticism is the occupational hazard for all Christians (1 Timothy 4:11–12, 6:20) and discouragement is a cancer of the spirit. We have to learn to be resistant to discouragement and hypercriticism. We are to learn to let the Holy Spirit encourage us more and more. Therefore, we need to be unencumbered by the things that can weigh us down (Hebrews 12:1–2).

We are to continually learn about being a servant to all we meet, acknowledging that the first shall be last and the last shall be first (Matthew 20:16). Priority is be given to serving all people we come into contact with, without favouritism or prejudice. An essential part of the Christian developing character is serving. If Jesus could be a humble servant, in that He came to earth as a member of His own creation, then we can also be identified as a humble servants willing to serve all.

> [25] Jesus called them together and said, 'You know that the rulers of the Gentiles lord it over them, and their high officials exercise authority over them. [26] Not so with you. Instead, whoever wants to become great among you must be your servant, [27] and whoever wants to be first must be your slave – [28] just as the Son of Man did not come to be served, but to serve, and to give His life as a ransom for many.' (Matthew 20:25–28)

We then go on to show that we are to be teachable because we have an unlimited ceiling of what we can be taught. A key part of our being a Christian, is a willingness to be taught by other people. When we are confronted by doubts or suffering, we are to persevere.

We can persevere by remembering that all Christians are linked together in a Christian community, which exists only through our relationship with Christ. There is no such thing as an individual member of the radical Christian community. We are to be interdependent upon one another, bound by a corporate and inclusive personality. The church community is to be dynamic by nature, and ever encouraging each other to push on in our faith.

We remember to persevere and overcome, in the strength and wisdom of the Holy Spirit, because He perseveres with us.

Section C: Weapon of Memory

Encouragement From Other Sojourners

Although the Christian cannot answer every question concerning faith in Christ and all that is going on in the world, Christians know God. They have believed in Him, and are convinced that He will keep throughout life, through death and eternity.[70]

We suffer much, but our hopes are great; we are exposed to snares and perils, but to save us we have not man but God. Our Saviour is not weak, for He is God, and whatever be our dangers they will not overcome us; nor is our hope made ashamed, for it is Christ. For in two ways we are enabled to bear up against dangers, when we are either speedily delivered from them, or supposed by good hopes under them.[71]

We may not understand where he leads us, or why things happen to others or to ourselves. Yet we must reaffirm the total trustworthiness of God, and our secure knowledge of his goodness and commitment to us. Remember that Christ died for you, that the Son of God willingly laid down his life for you.[72]

---

[70] Carswell, 142
[71] Chrysostom, Page 704
[72] McGrath, Page 132

Engaged in Battle

C8. We Remain Committed

²¹ 'Not everyone who says to me, "Lord, Lord," will enter the kingdom of heaven, but only the one who does the will of my Father who is in heaven. ²² Many will say to me on that day, "Lord, Lord, did we not prophesy in your name and in your name drive out demons and in your name perform many miracles?" ²³ Then I will tell them plainly, "I never knew you. Away from me, you evildoers!"

²⁴ 'Therefore everyone who hears these words of mine and puts them into practice is like a wise man who built His house on the rock. ²⁵ The rain came down, the streams rose, and the winds blew and beat against that house; yet it did not fall, because it had its foundation on the rock. ²⁶ But everyone who hears these words of mine and does not put them into practice is like a foolish man who built His house on sand. ²⁷ The rain came down, the streams rose, and the winds blew and beat against that house, and it fell with a great crash.'

²⁸ When Jesus had finished saying these things, the crowds were amazed at His teaching, ²⁹ because He taught as one who had authority, and not as their teachers of the law.
(Matthew 7:21–29)

Up until now, Jesus has been issuing instructions. It is here, therefore, that He issues the two choices people face when having heard His words. He concludes His sermon with a heart–wrenching application. Jesus confronts us with Himself and sets before us the choice between obeying His words or disobeying them. He then proceeds to call us to firm commitment of mind, will & life to Himself and His teaching. Jesus warns of the mere spoken profession (Matthew 7:21–23), and the dangers of a mere intellectual knowledge without any practical knowledge (Matthew 7:24–27). Each one of these, is a substitute for the

Section C: Weapon of Memory

obedience that Jesus requires, asks for and commands of all those who would follow Him.

These final two passages are very similar. Both contrast the right & wrong responses to Jesus & His teaching. Both show a definite decision must be made; and that nothing replaces an active and practical obedience to Him. The only difference between the passages, is that the first is to people who only say they are Christians and the second is to people who only have an intellectual acceptance of Jesus and His teachings.

The people that Jesus refers to here, are those that say they belong to Him, but in practice do nothing to change their lives in accordance to His teachings. Not all who say to Jesus, "Lord, Lord" will enter the kingdom of heaven (Matthew 7:21). A person's final destiny will be settled, Jesus says, neither by what we say to Him today nor on the last day, but whether we practice what He teaches and obey Him.

> [8] But what does it say? 'The word is near you; it is in your mouth and in your heart,' that is, the message concerning faith that we proclaim: [9] if you declare with your mouth, 'Jesus is Lord,' and believe in your heart that God raised Him from the dead, you will be saved. [10] For it is with your heart that you believe and are justified, and it is with your mouth that you profess your faith and are saved. [11] As Scripture says, 'Anyone who believes in Him will never be put to shame.' (Romans 10:8–11)

We are to confess with our lips and believe in our hearts. A true profession of Jesus is impossible without the Holy Spirit (1 Corinthians 12:3). Is there anything wrong with calling Jesus, "Lord"? In itself, no. However, if there is no moral & practical application, then it is merely lip service and is worth nothing. People who do not talk with truth, and profess Jesus without reality, will not be saved. People who only live a verbal confession of Jesus can be full of courtesy, enthusiasm and orthodoxy in private worship and public ministry and yet live without any of the moral teachings of Jesus. Look at the list given here of prophecy, casting out demons and doing mighty works in His name (Matthew 7:21–29). Yet, if those people do not do the will of the Father, and obey the teachings of Jesus, then they too will be told to depart from Jesus. These three areas of ministry: prophecy, exorcism and miracles are the most extreme examples of verbal professions, and yet if these people do not obey Jesus, then they will be cast away from the presence of Jesus. Jesus is not just for their lips, but for their whole life as well. Jesus is not just for them to say, "We follow him!" and yet not do as He asks. That is merely paying lip service. It is for them to say they follow Jesus and to do as He has commanded them to do.

The difference is between saying they do it and actually doing it. Those who pay lip service to God, may claim to do mighty works in ministry, but in everyday behaviour the works done are not good, but evil. Those who claim to be followers of Jesus, have made a profession of Christ in their private conversations and publicly in their baptism. They appear to honour Jesus by referring to Him as "the Lord", or "our Lord". They say the Lord's prayer in church, and sing songs expressing their love to Jesus. They may even teach in the name of Jesus, of mention and use His name in other areas of ministry in the church.

Jesus, however, is not impressed by words, but wants those who claim to follow Him, to do as He has commanded them to do. To be committed to Jesus, is for Christians to do the will of God the Father. He asks for evidence of our sincerity in good works of obedience, as one of His followers wherever we go.

Where the contrast in the last passage was between "saying" and "doing", the contrast is now between "hearing" and "doing". On one hand Jesus says that there is this person who hears these words of His and does them (Matthew 7:24), and on the other hand, the person who hears the words of Jesus and does not do them (Matthew 7:26).

To give a clearer idea, of what the contrasts are, Jesus tells a parable about two builders. The man, who built & constructed His house on

Section C: Weapon of Memory

deeply dug rock is, according to Jesus, wise. Yet, the man who built His house on sand without laying a solid foundation is foolish, according to Jesus. As both men were building, anyone passing by probably would not have noticed any difference between them. Why? Because the difference was their foundations, and foundations cannot be seen. Only after the storm, floods and high winds, was the basic and fatal difference able to be seen. For the house that was built on rock, remained standing, whereas the house built upon sand was destroyed forever.

In the same way, people who say they are Christians often look the same, whether they are genuine or fake. It is hard to tell. Both appear to be building solid Christian lives. For Jesus is not comparing professing Christians with non–Christians. What is common to both spiritual housebuilders is that they hear these words of Jesus. Both are members of the Christian church. Both read the Bible, go to church, listen to sermons and read Christian books. The reason why nobody cannot tell the difference between them, is because the foundations are buried deep and are invisible. The question is not whether these people hear the word of Jesus, but whether they are obedient and doing the word of Jesus. Only a storm can show the truth. A storm of crisis or trouble reveals what kind of person we really are. How do we face up to the everyday trials of life? Do we hold up to the values expressed in the Sermon on the Mount, or do we just act like we used to do before we became a Christian?

The truth that Jesus would have us learn from these two passages, is that a mere intellectual knowledge or verbal acknowledgement can substitute for obedience to His word. The question is not whether we say nice, polite, enthusiastic things to or about Jesus; nor whether we hear His words, listening, studying, pondering and memorising until our minds are stuffed full of His teaching; but whether we do what we say and put into practise what we know to be truth. In other words, is the lordship of Jesus truly a reality in our life?

However, this is not teaching that salvation comes through good works or good deeds. Nor is it the way to enter the kingdom of heaven, by good works of obedience, because the whole New Testament offers salvation through the grace of God through faith in Jesus Christ and Him alone. Here Jesus stresses that those who truly hear the gospel and profess faith in Him will obey Him, and therefore expressing their faith by their works. It is in applying this teaching to our lives, that we can consider the reading of the Bible and belonging to the world–wide church. For if we do both of these things, then we have a serious responsibility to ensure that what we know, and what we say is translated into what we do, and how we live.

Jesus places radical and life changing choices before us. He commands us to be real followers of Himself, joining a new culture, the Christian culture, which has abandoned the old culture of the world. He repeatedly called His followers to be different from the world. We are to be salt and light, in a bland and dark world (Matthew 5:13–16). Spiritually, the world around us is like rotting food that is full of bacteria causing it to decay rapidly. As the followers of Jesus, we are to be salt, stopping this decay and deterioration. The world lives in spiritual darkness, a gloomy, dank & shadowy place. As Christian ambassadors, we are called to be light, throwing out the darkness & gloom.

Our righteousness is to be so deep that it reaches our heart, and our love is to be so wide as to cover everyone including our enemies. Our giving, our prayers and fasting are not to be as the Pharisees were in boasting, but rather to be real, and in secret, so as not to compromise our Christian integrity. For our treasure, we are to choose what lasts through all eternity, not that which rots away here on earth. We are to have as our master, God, and not money or possessions. Our ambitions should not be our own material security, but the spread of God's rule & righteousness in the world. Our heavenly Father is a peacemaker and loves even those who are ungrateful and selfish. As Christians, we are commanded to do the same, emulating Him. By doing so, we then show to the world, and to God, that we are truly His children (Matthew 5:9, 44–48). We are offered the choice, either to follow the crowd in the world or to follow our Father in heaven. We are given the choice of being ruled by the opinions of the world or being mastered by God's word. We are either for Him or against Him.

We have two ways to go, a narrow or broad gate, and two foundations we can build, either on rock or on sand. The narrow gate built on rock, is the path to life, while the broad gate built on sand leads to death, decay and destruction. The answer to these choices is important and certainly much more important than our careers or marriage partner. Which road shall we travel on, and upon which foundation shall we build our house? Those who decide for Jesus, choose the narrow gate, and a firm foundation in Jesus.

CARRY AND COUNT

> "Whoever wants to be my disciple must deny themselves and take up their cross daily and follow me. For whoever wants to save their life will lose it, but whoever loses their life for me will save it. What good is it for someone to gain the whole world, and yet lose or forfeit their very self? Whoever is ashamed of me and my words, the Son of Man will be ashamed of them when He comes in His glory and in the glory of the Father and of the holy angels." (Luke 9:23–26)

As a sign of the Christian's commitment to God and following Jesus, here is where the rubber hits the road, as it were. These were the words of Jesus, and most certainly were some of the most challenging that He said. Carry a cross? That must have been just about the most degrading thing anybody could possibly ask anyone to do in those days. And not only degrading, also incredibly painful as it would have followed a terrible scourging and been followed by the most terrible death. Did Jesus really mean what He said? It seems so because the historical record suggests that Peter died that way, crucified upside down. The apostle James had it easy by comparison – He was beheaded (Acts 12:2)! What is our response to that to be?

As Christians, we are being commanded to count the cost of following Him. That is how we carry our own cross for the sake of Jesus Christ. Jesus wants to be number one in our life as we follow Him. Jesus wants supremacy over everything in our life, including family, friends, and possessions.

Alas, that's a cost too high for some. Matthew relates the story where a man runs up to Jesus and wants eternal life, wants it now and asks Jesus about how to get it (Matthew 19:16–25). This man has fully kept the commandments listed by Jesus. However, when Jesus said to the man that to follow Him, He would have to give up all His wealth and possessions in order to have treasure in heaven and eternal life, the man leaves disconsolate and shattered. The life of this man reflected a life of absorption with His own self–interest and self–importance. It was a step too far for Him. He wanted His riches and also everlasting life, but Jesus said He couldn't have both. He remains the only person that is known to have left Jesus' presence with such sorrow. That was due to His putting all His trust in Himself , His riches and wealth alone. Now riches, in and of themselves, are not necessarily wrong. But for this rich young man, He was not willing to make the sacrifice required to follow Jesus. He couldn't count the cost of following Jesus – it was too high a price for Him to pay.

What have we given up as a result of our decision to follow Jesus? What in future will we have to give up in order to continue following Jesus Christ? Making sacrifices to follow Jesus is all part of having life with Jesus. Jesus, who is our Lord, Master and King, demands that He be number one and supreme over everything else in our life, including our own self, our family, other people and material goods including money and possessions. How can this task be completed?

It is achieved by constantly ensuring that our works and words match our lifestyle, and that no hypocrisy can be found, or will be found, in our life. It means standing up for God in the face of adversity. It means loving others even though they hate us. Here in England, we are not systematically persecuted. We may at times be marginalized, ridiculed and ignored.

But this is not being actively persecuted, unlike in some other parts of the world, where members of the Christian family face death daily, simply because they choose to follow Jesus. They are carrying their cross for Jesus and counting the cost of following Him? If we were known by others because of our self-sacrificial love of all others, then Jesus whom we claim to love, follow, worship, and adore, would inevitably be seen. A Christian is a person who has taken up their own cross in following Jesus and counting the cost of being a disciple of Jesus Christ.

> "[24] Then Jesus said to his disciples, 'Whoever wants to be my disciple must deny themselves and take up their cross and follow me. [25] For whoever wants to save their life will lose it, but whoever loses their life for me will find it. [26] What good will it be for someone to gain the whole world, yet forfeit their soul? Or what can anyone give in exchange for their soul? [27] For the Son of Man is going to come in his Father's glory with his angels, and then he will reward each person according to what they have done. (Matthew 16:24–27)

Jesus tells all those who choose to follow Him, to take up their own cross if they are to follow Him and be His disciple. How is that possible? If we try to do that in our own strength and wisdom, we will fail. If we do it using the power and strength of the Holy Spirit within us, then we will succeed at following Jesus' command. Are we as disciples of Jesus Christ willing to take up our cross and count the cost of following Him?

What a difference that would make to the communities and nations where we live, if all who claimed to be Christians were living like that!

We remember to remain committed to God, carrying our own cross and being obedient to Him wholeheartedly.

Section C: Weapon of Memory

Encouragement From Other Sojourners

Take up your cross, therefore, and follow Jesus, and you shall enter eternal life. He Himself opened the way before you in carrying His cross, and upon it He died for you, that you, too, might take up your cross and long to die upon it.[73]

God as a human in the form of Jesus could be received or rejected, cared for or abused, nurtured or stifled, loved or hated. This is the way Jesus came into this world and this is also the way he sends us. … sent in the way Jesus was, we as his followers might be received, though on the other hand we might easily be rejected; we might be cared for but equally we may be abused; we may be welcomed with open arms and loved, or just as readily we might be hated.[74]

He warned people to 'count the cost' before becoming Christians. 'Make no mistake,' He says, 'if you let me, I will make you perfect. The moment you put yourself in My hands, that is what you are in for. Nothing less, or other, than that.'[75]

Yet the Christian life is not easy, nor is it meant to be. Jesus himself pointed out that following in his footsteps involved taking up a cross. To be a Christian is potentially to suffer. As Christians down the ages have discovered, the quality of Christian witness is directly proportional to the extent to which the Church is persecuted.[76]

---

[73] à Kempis, Page 57
[74] Drane, Page 132
[75] Lewis01, Page 202
[76] McGrath, Page 9

C9. We Will Be With Others

[19] Therefore, brothers and sisters, since we have confidence to enter the Most Holy Place by the blood of Jesus, [20] by a new and living way opened for us through the curtain, that is, His body, [21] and since we have a great priest over the house of God, [22] let us draw near to God with a sincere heart and with the full assurance that faith brings, having our hearts sprinkled to cleanse us from a guilty conscience and having our bodies washed with pure water. [23] Let us hold unswervingly to the hope we profess, for He who promised is faithful. [24] And let us consider how we may spur one another on towards love and good deeds, [25] not giving up meeting together, as some are in the habit of doing, but encouraging one another – and all the more as you see the Day approaching.
(Hebrews 10:19–25)

One of the greatest blessings of our being a Christian, is fellowship with other Christian believers. It is because fellowship results from Christians walking with one another (1 John 1:7). Walking with one another with Jesus Christ in the very centre. The Church is a gathering of people, engaging in human activities with human customs, texts, orders, procedures and possessions through the power of God the Holy Spirit.

God has created people for fellowship – both with Himself and with other humans. We are in need of other people for all sorts of reasons. Jesus Christ has redeemed us so that we can have true fellowship together with other Christians (Colossians 1:3–5). What do we mean by the words 'fellowship'? Fellowship is rooted in the New Testament words *'koinōnia'* and *'koinōneō'*, which are defined as a mutual sharing together, and not just a mere mutual association. Fellowship is both in having fellowship and giving fellowship.

Section C: Weapon of Memory

When we fellowship with other Christians, God is glorified (Romans 15:7). It is when we are involved with a collective body that a Church fellowship grows in grace and maturity together, overcoming by grace, the weaknesses of each individual member (Ephesians 4:11–16). We are commanded to continue meeting others for fellowship, so that mutual encouragement and exhortation "towards love and good deeds" can take place (Hebrews 10:24–25).

As we do this, we can live a consistent godly life, particularly if sins are confessed to each other (James 5:16), so that prayer for healing can take place between us. Victory is also seen in the eyes of a fellowship, rather than the individual person (1 Corinthians 15:57; 1 John 5:4). Additionally, New Testament exhortations to live holy lives are said to groups of Christians (Romans 6:1–23) and victory is also seen in the eyes of a fellowship or community, rather than singular individuals (1 Corinthians 15:57; 1 John 4:11, 5:4).

Whilst God does indeed deal with us as individuals, it is through fellowship that God strengthens us, for we are supported, healed and encouraged by other Christians. Biblical fellowship sees Christians exhibiting these characteristics. The body of Christian believers, the Church, show that they have a common purpose (Psalm 133:1–3; Philippians 1:3–6), belief (Acts 2:42), hope (Hebrews 11:39–40) and needs (2 Corinthians 8:1–15)

Just as we as Christians have fellowship with God the Father (1 John 1:3), Jesus (1 Corinthians 1:9), the Holy Spirit (Philippians 2:1), we also have fellowship with other Christian believers (1 John 1:7). The things that our fellowship with other Christians share include our possessions (2 Corinthians 8:4), our sufferings (Philippians 3:10) and the Gospel (Galatians 2:9; Philippians 1:5).

As part of being with other people, we are to tell other people about Jesus. Moreover, as we show love to other Christians, we are engaged in evangelism because we will be showing that we are a follower of Jesus (John 13:35).

Lord's Supper

> "He took bread, gave thanks and broke it, and gave it to them [the disciples], saying, "This is my body given for you; do this in remembrance of me."
> In the same way, after the supper He took the cup, saying, "This cup is the new covenant in my blood, which is poured out for you." (Luke 22:19–20)

This meal is called amongst other things, Holy Communion, the Eucharist or The Lord's Supper. Christians are commanded to participate in this central act of corporate worship. Some Churches do it every service and others do it monthly. Whenever we participate in it, we are to do it regularly as a remembrance of Jesus until He comes again (1 Corinthians 11:26). This is of course, another facet of the memory being a spiritual weapon.

The bread symbolizes Jesus' body broken on the cross. The wine symbolizes His blood shed on the cross. Therefore, before we partake of the bread and wine, we are to examine ourselves and confess to God any unforgiven sin in our life (1 Corinthians 11:28–29). This is done because it would be hypocritical of us to eat the bread and drink the wine, harbouring known sin in our heart while endeavouring to have fellowship with Jesus and other Christian believers. The Lord's Supper symbolizes the death of Jesus Christ for our sin (Luke 22:19). It reflects our acceptance of Jesus Christ's death for us. It shows our total dependence upon Him for spiritual life and our having observably fellowshipped with others (1 Corinthians 10:17).

In engaging with this sacrament of the Lord's Supper, we have received the benefits of His sacrifice (1 Corinthians 10:16) and have spiritually fed upon Jesus Christ (1 Corinthians 11:24). This also acts as a reminder of all that Jesus Christ means to us (1 Corinthians 11:25), as it reflects the New Covenant between God and us, as Christian believers. This New Covenant which is the consummate guarantee of salvation for us and for all those who are following Jesus Christ, as we remember the significance of Jesus' death and resurrection on our life.

LOVE

> "Whoever claims to love God yet hates a brother or sister is a liar. For whoever does not love their brother and sister, whom they have seen, cannot love God, whom they have not seen." (1 John 4:20)

Jesus commands that all those who declare that they love Him, should also go and love their enemies (Matthew 5:43–48). Jesus commanded His followers, all those who claimed to be His disciples, to love those they didn't like or were ever going to like. As Christians, we are to actively love all other people. It is very difficult to show love to others if we are never in the company of others.

The world around us in the media and elsewhere, the assumption is that towards our enemies, we are to be confrontational or at best just ignore them. How is it possible to love our enemies? It is only with the help of God and His abundant grace towards us, as we depend on the Holy Spirit to empower us. By relying on the power and strength of the Holy Spirit living within us, we can love all people – including our enemies. To love only those who love us, is what those outside the Church expect as normal behaviour. But as Christians, we are to be seen to love others – all others.

As Christians, we are to be radically different from other humans, in that we are to love extraordinarily and extravagantly, compelled, as we are to reflect our love for God through loving other people. We don't have to like other people as friends, but we do have to love them as fellow humans. What kind of love is this? Is it a friendly love or perhaps a romantic love? Certainly not. It is an *agape* love. *Agape* is one of the four Greek words for love. It was used more in Scripture than anywhere else, so it can understandably be taken to be the peculiarly Christian sort of love. This is a love which is sacrificial and self–less. This is not a soppy plastic Hollywood love. This is tough love which is the very giving of one's very self in order that the Christian is of service to other people regardless of any relationship between them. We are to love others sacrificially, and thereby echo the very way that God loved and continues to love us.

As Christians, we should be so filled and magnetized with God's love and grace, that it is a magnetic attraction to others of the majestic goodness and love of God. By loving others in this way, the Gospel becomes attractive and undeniable. The prime hallmark of being a Christian is to love. Can we run out of this type of love? No! Why not? Because it is always topped up by the grace of the God. Amazing love!

SERVING

We can show this love by serving, for service is fundamental to the Christian life. Serving God and other people is a fundamental hallmark of a spiritually mature Christian. For it is through serving, that we, as Christians, reflect the greatest servant of all, Jesus Christ, and His great love for humanity. For Jesus Christ came to serve and to give His life for others (Mark 10:45).

As Christians, we are to be as Jesus Christ and to serve all other people. Yet if we are honest, we sometimes feel incapable. That is because we forget that God the Holy Spirit is within us to empower us to obediently serve God and serve others. The Christian life is to be a very practical way of life.

As Christians, partakers of Jesus Christ, we are called to a life of service. The Church is to be a body of people, where each person is to have a serving function – serving God and serving others. Why are we to serve others? When we serve with others as a Church, or indeed with

Section C: Weapon of Memory

a group of Churches, this shows unity and solidarity to those outside of the Church who frequently accuse the Church of infighting and "devouring one another". Our Christian life is not to be static or inactive, but rather it is to be dynamic and active. The word 'servant' is key in Scripture. It is used at least five hundred times in its various derivations. Spiritual growth comes from serving, rather than being served.

This is because whatever is given in service of God and others makes faith and Jesus Christ gives back even more. Jesus recounts a parable highlighting the rewards for faithful service and the penalties for being faithless (Matthew 25:14–30). Serving others is a sign that we are trusting God and that we are showing faith in Him. Showing love and serving others shows obedience to Jesus Christ. As a part of the Church, we are dependent upon others, just as one part of the human body is dependent on another part. That is why we are serve others and use the gifts generously given to us by God, and so that God received the glory, praise and honour, as the Kingdom is built.

> Each of you should use whatever gift you have received to serve
> others, as faithful stewards of God's grace in its various forms.
> (1 Peter 4:10)

When we, as Christians and partakers of Jesus Christ, serve in any capacity, then God's honour is released. This is because service shows the beauty and glory of Jesus Christ to both those being served and those watching on. That is to be our motive for service. Serving should never to be about what we can get out of it. When that is the motive, God is patently not glorified. God's glory and supremacy is to be the goal of all those who would call themselves Christians. As Jesus said:

> "Very truly I tell you, whoever believes in me will do the works
> I have been doing, and they will do even greater things than
> these, because I am going to the Father."
> (John 14:12)

When Jesus said these words to His apostles, it was through the promised Holy Spirit (John 14:17), and the impartment or widespread giving of Spiritual gifts, that His words were fulfilled. The phrase "spiritual gifts" derives from the Greek word *'charismata.'* They are also called grace gifts, because *'charis'* means grace and they refer to any gift God gives out of the abundance of His grace. They are given to all Christians as God sees fit (1 Corinthians 12:11). They are not all externally ecstatic spectacular gifts such as healing and tongues, as some Churches today propose. Not everybody will have one of those externally spectacular gifts. Some have to be content with much more everyday things like hospitality and giving.

The gifts quoted from the New Testament reflect this diversity (Romans 12:6–8; 1 Corinthians 12:8–10; 1 Corinthians 12:28–30; Ephesians 4:11; 1 Peter 4:11). They include gifts such as administration, apostleship, discernment, evangelism, exhortation, giving, faith, healing, helps, knowledge, leadership, mercy, miracles, pastor, prophecy, service, teaching, tongues, tongues interpretation, wisdom. Paul commands that Christians "try to excel in gifts that build up the Church" (1 Corinthians 14:12). There are probably many more gifts outside of this list. When the Church is built up, unity prevails, for the diversity of Spiritual gifts within each local Church, helps build unity.

All Christians have at least one spiritual gift. As Christians, we have spiritual gifts, for as Paul writes: "We have different gifts, according to the grace given to each of us" (Romans 12:6). God the Holy Spirit, through His infinite wisdom, mercy and grace bestows a gift or some gifts upon us to be used so that God is glorified through our service to Him (1 Peter 4:11). The reason that the Holy Spirit imparts spiritual gifts to us, is so that the whole body of Christ can be built up (Ephesians 4:12), for the common good of the Church (1 Corinthians 12:7, 14:12) and "so that in all things God may be praised through Jesus Christ" (1 Peter 4:11).

These reasons mean that God wants us to be active in service of Him

Section C: Weapon of Memory

and of all others. As Christians, we are dependent upon each other, just as one part of the human body has dependence on another part. That is why we are to serve other people and use the gifts generously given by God. All Christians have gifts and have a responsibility to discover and develop those gifts (1 Timothy 4:14). God has called us and equipped us with spiritual gifts, and they are not to be neglected. We are to discover, discern, develop and put into effect our spiritual gifts, so that God can and will be glorified, and His Church built up. We are to continue to ask God to facilitate their development and strengthening and give us opportunities to use them. We are to seek gifts that build up others, commands Paul (1 Corinthians 14:1–12).

One of those gifts is the gift of giving. Paul lists giving as a spiritual gift (Romans 12:6–8). Every person has time, possessions and money in differing quantities. These things in and of themselves are not evil. The whole Christian community is one that is to reflect the God whom we love, follow serve and are obedient to. The Church is to be a community where the strongest members support the weakest members. This applies not only to the local Church, but also to the universal Church and therefore has a national and international context to it as well. Too often, Christians are found to be turning a blind eye to the suffering of others where the bare necessities of life are in sparse existence.

Perhaps the greatest indicator of the spiritual growth of a Christian is in the area of financial giving. Paul, writing to the Corinthian Church, commands that giving be done whole–heartedly and cheerfully (2 Corinthians 9:7). It is not so much how much is given, but how much is left after giving. God looks beyond the amount that is given to the motive behind the giving. All of our money and possessions belong to God anyway, so giving is to be in response to this. Giving is to be done out of love for God. Paul offers a three–point system for giving, where it is to be regular, methodical and proportionate (1 Corinthians 16:2).

Failure to give back to God's work what He has given the Christian in the first place, robs God (Malachi 3:8). The reason it robs is because the giving cannot be used to support those who are working for God. As a result of giving, the Christian disciple will be blessed (Malachi 3:10) and have their needs satisfied (Philippians 4:19). During the Old Testament days, widows and the struggling were important to God. Why so? Because justice is important to God. He is a God of justice and mercy.

The Apostles would have known all that about God caring for the widows and would have heard Jesus' teaching about justice for the poor and the oppressed. The outworking of this is seen in the early Church where people were selling and sharing possessions and ensuring that people within the Christian community were being looked after and cared for (Acts 2:42–47; Acts 4:32–36). This included making sure that everyone got fed, particularly those who had no family to care for them. This was not just for those in the Church, but included those who were not Christians and not in the Church.

We remember to be with others, including those who, for whatever reason, are not able to get out.

Section C: Weapon of Memory

Encouragement From Other Sojourners

But as the Divine nature is of higher excellence than, and far removed above, our nature, the command to love God is distinct from that to love our neighbour. For He shows us pity on account of His own goodness, but we show pity to one another on account of His;—that is, He pities us that we may fully enjoy Himself; we pity one another that we may fully enjoy Him.[77]

What we have to remind ourselves in our Western individualistic society, is that to comprehend and experience the love of Christ in all its fullness, has a corporate dimension to it.[78]

The early Christians, living as they did in a dangerous world where they were surrounded by all kinds of threats and where life expectancy was relatively short, were given strength to live as sacrificially as they did, contributing much to the wellbeing of others, by the fact that they had a real and living hope that went beyond the grave.[79]

The enemy does not feel compassion when Christians fall; he is prowling around looking for people to devour (1 Peter 5:8). The sad truth is that so many in the church are listening to and choosing to believe the lies rather than believing the truth about who God says they are.[80]

---

[77] Augustine, Page 42
[78] Christou, Page 57
[79] Lennox, Page 56
[80] Mann, Page 54

C10. We Worship God Only

> ¹ Give praise to the LORD, proclaim His name; make known among the nations what He has done.
> ² Sing to him, sing praise to him; tell of all His wonderful acts.
> ³ Glory in His holy name;
> let the hearts of those who seek the LORD rejoice.
> ⁴ Look to the LORD and His strength; seek His face always.
> ⁵ Remember the wonders He has done,
> his miracles, and the judgments He pronounced,
> ⁶ you His servants, the descendants of Abraham,
> his chosen ones, the children of Jacob.
> ⁷ He is the LORD our God;
> his judgments are in all the earth.
> (Psalm 105:1–7)

Now to another of our weapons, which is also a facet of our memory weapon. We remember to worship God! Worshipping God, where through the use of our mind, emotions and senses, we direct all honour and respect only towards God, in the power and direction of the Holy Spirit and in truth.

> "Yet a time is coming and has now come when the true worshippers will worship the Father in the Spirit and in truth, for they are the kind of worshippers the Father seeks. God is spirit, and His worshippers must worship in the Spirit and in truth.'" (John 4:23–24)

Worshipping in Spirit involves the whole person – mind, body and will. Worshipping in truth means that all true worship reflects God's character. Worshipping with other Christians should be an intimate, dynamic and holy encounter with God. How often does that happen in Churches today?

Section C: Weapon of Memory

Why do we worship God? We worship God because God commands us to worship Him (1 Chronicles 16:29). God deserves our worship, for He alone personifies goodness (Psalm 100:4–5), holiness (Psalm 99:5, 9), mercy (Exodus 4:31) and power (Revelation 4:11). God is to be worshipped in obedience to Him as our Creator (Revelation 4:11) and as our Lord and Saviour (Habakkuk 3:18). Worship should bring satisfaction to all parts of us (Romans 12:2; Colossians 3:24).

Worshipping with others in a Church is worship. But it is only part of worship, and certainly not the full meaning of worship. Worship is to include obedience and submission to God. Worship is not just to be on Sunday, or through individual acts during the rest of the week. Worship for the Christian is to be an active dynamic relationship with Jesus Christ seeking a life of total obedience and submission to Him.

True worship of the living God involves total obedience to His ways and not just singing songs. For the ancient Israelites, sacrifices were an innate part of their life and worship structure. Yet as Samuel said: "To obey is better than sacrifice, and to heed is better than the fat of rams." (1 Samuel 15:22)

What he is saying there, is that God prefers whole life obedience rather than acts of worship. Obedience and submission to God are true worship of Him. Seeking to obey Him and submit our life to Him is true worship of Him. Worship is to be to God alone. Yet sometimes preachers and other Church leaders can be raised to an unhealthy status, with a sort of reverence which is unbiblical. It is as if they are being worshipped, and not God. God alone is to be worshipped. Christians are exhorted and encouraged to submit to and be obedient to God, in all aspects of life, as an act of adoring and loving worship of and to God alone.

One of the very essential growth elements for Christians along with prayer and Bible reading is the requirement to worship publicly. There is a meaning of worship, whereby our very life is to be a spiritual act of worship (Romans 12:1). However, by worship, we mean public acts of worship, such as in a Church or chapel service. When worshipping God, we are to give all respect, honour and glory to God. When this is done in reverence, in truth and in submission to the Lord Jesus Christ, then as Christians, we continue to mature and grow spiritually. Why do we Christians worship? Perhaps the greatest reason that we worship is because God commands it. The Ten Commandments (Exodus 20:1–3) insist that God alone is worshipped, adored and paid homage to. As human beings we are made in His image and as Christians , He owns us because we claim Jesus to be our Lord and Master. So, it is right and just that we give worship to this God who paid the penalty for sin, so that we may be His child, and He wants us to honour His desire that we should call Him Father. We discover an inner personal satisfaction when God is worshipped and adored, both for the present and in the future (Romans 12:2; Colossians 3:24).

Another reason to give worship to God alone is that God deserves our worship. All of God's attributes demand that we revere and worship Him. His holiness, goodness, love, mercy and providence are but a beginning as to why He, and He alone, is worthy of our worship. It is by His twin wellsprings of grace and mercy that we worship Him.

Worship is a way for us to give supreme honour and reverence to God, through our actions, words, attitudes and thoughts. As Christians, we acknowledge that God Almighty alone is worthy of our reverence, submission and worship. There are many other things that are worshipped and thus are 'gods', with a small 'g'. Money, careers, possessions and other people are 21st century examples of things which are worshipped by humans.

The threat of materialism is a huge danger to Christians, because the worship of material possessions takes the supreme place of worship to God, and some Christians have been duped by it. The Bible clearly states that God alone is to be worshipped. For God is to carry the worshipping Christian disciple, and not the Christian to carry the 'god'. We gather with other people in expectation of meeting God and that He will receive the worship and praise which He alone is due. As part of public worship with others there are the sacraments of Baptism and Holy Communion. Baptism is where we publicly identified with the death, burial and resurrection of Jesus Christ. I look back to the early 1980s and my own Baptism. I can see how God has worked upon me and grown me since that day of public affirmation by me concerning the greatness of Jesus Christ. Holy Communion is where we participate regularly as a Christian and remember Jesus' death for our sin, accept His death for us, and our dependence upon Him in His resurrection for our spiritual life.

Another element of public worship is the reading and preaching of the Bible. This is where God's word is read in public. Then God's Word is preached so that God's word can be applied to the hearer's lives. The whole of a Church worship service should be where the spiritually comfortable are discomforted and those spiritually uncomfortable are comforted. Worship should be where non–Christians who are present can honestly and openly proclaim, that "God is really among us." Sometimes we need to worship God with others, even if we don't feel like it and pray for God to help us worship Him with other people, our Church family. Public worship is for encouragement of the worshipping group of believers and not for the individual worshipper. Overall, the Apostle Paul plainly encourages:

"Everything that is done must be useful to all and build them up in the Lord" (1 Corinthians 14:26).

However, there are frequent warnings in the Bible about the sin of idolatry. I wonder if when you hear that word "idolatry", you instantly imagine somebody bowing before a statue and worshipping it. A good example is the story of the Israelites worshipping the golden calf, as recorded by Moses (Exodus 32). Or perhaps in our own time when we see people bowing down to the statue of the Buddha or one of the many Hindu gods. Therefore, we tend to think that idolatry is worshipping statues or worshipping in other religions such as Islam, Jainism and Zoroastrianism.

However, the Bible is very clear, particularly in what Jesus said, that idolatry is a threat to living and partaking in the Christian life. As Christians, we are to love God and love others. Anything that replaces our love of God as our first priority, is an idol, and therefore, is idolatry. For idolatry is not merely worshipping statues. It is much more than that. Idolatry is the transference of allegiance to something, anything, apart from God. Idolatry is worshipping created things or people, and not worshipping God the Father through Jesus Christ the Son of God in the power of the indwelling God the Holy Spirit. Idolatry can be with anything, for anything can take first place in our life instead of God. It may be our car, our family, our Church, a Christian leader, entertainment, celebrities and even ourselves.

These are all good things, in and of themselves, but they are not good things if they replace God from first priority in our life. These things can turn out to be idols, because they relegate our thinking of Almighty God to below first place. Idolatry is primarily a sin of the mind. How so?

> [18] "The wrath of God is being revealed from heaven against all the godlessness and wickedness of people, who suppress the truth by their wickedness, [19] since what may be known about God is plain to them, because God has made it plain to them. [20] For since the creation of the world God's invisible qualities – His eternal power and divine nature – have been clearly seen, being understood from what has been made, so that people are without excuse.
>
> [21] For although they knew God, they neither glorified Him as God nor gave thanks to him, but their thinking became futile and their foolish hearts were darkened. [22] Although they claimed to be wise, they became fools [23] and exchanged the glory of the immortal God for images made to look like a mortal

Section C: Weapon of Memory

> human being and birds and animals and reptiles. ²⁴ Therefore God gave them over in the sinful desires of their hearts to sexual impurity for the degrading of their bodies with one another. ²⁵ They exchanged the truth about God for a lie, and worshipped and served created things rather than the Creator – who is for ever praised. Amen." (Romans 1:18–25)

Paul elucidates, that although people knew God, they neither glorified Him as God nor did they give thanks to Him. Rather, their thinking became utterly futile and their foolish hearts were darkened. Although people claimed to be wise, they became fools and exchanged the glory of the immortal God for images made to look like a mortal human being and birds and animals and reptiles.

Therefore, God gave them over in the sinful desires of their hearts to sexual impurity for the degrading of their bodies with one another. They exchanged the truth about God for a lie and worshipped and served created things rather than the Creator – who is for ever praised. Here, Paul links idolatry with immorality. Immorality is the outer sin and idolatry is the inward sin.

Idolatry is an attitude within a person that says to God, "You are not first place; this other person or thing is". If we commit the sin of idolatry, then we are a slave to that something else and we will not be a slave to God through Jesus Christ in the power of the Holy Spirit. Idolatry is not just worshipping in another religion and bowing down to statues. Idolatry is also when relegating God to second place, in both actions and attitudes.

Consequently, we are to cast off anything that is blocking our relationship with Almighty God. As idolatry is primarily the sin of the mind, those depraved ideas turn to sins of lusts and idolatrous physical pleasures. As we are renewed in our thinking and have a renewed mind, we can worship Almighty God through Jesus Christ the Lord, in the power of the Holy Spirit. With that said, can our view and experience of worship sometimes be too small? Indeed it can be, particularly when the worship we offer, is not giving God alone the glory which is due His name in the splendour of His holiness (Psalm 19:2).

We remember to give whole life worship to God alone.

Section C: Weapon of Memory

Encouragement From Other Sojourners

The word, to worship, means to stoop and bow down the body with external gestures; to serve in the work. But to worship God in spirit is the service and honour of the heart; it comprehends faith and fear in God. The worshipping of God is two–fold, outward and inward — that is, to acknowledge God's benefits, and to be thankful unto him.[81]

Worship refreshes us, precisely because it forces us to raise our eyes upwards and appreciate the immensity and grandeur of our maker and redeemer. And excited and invigorated by this vision, we return to the Christian life with a new sense of commitment and renewed energy.[82]

Worship is the opening of my heart to the love of God, it is the coming of a child to His Father., it is drawing near to love and to adore.[83]

We must celebrate all the goodness of the world, all of God's goodness to us in creation. But we must not worship it. We must thank God for it – and pray and watch for the day when it will be transformed by the royal appearing of his son.[84]

---

[81] Luther, Page 410
[82] McGrath, Page 61
[83] Watson, Page 120
[84] Wright, Page 147

A Final Word

As part of Christ's army, you march in the ranks of gallant spirits. Every one of your fellow soldiers is the child of a King. Some, like you, are in the midst of the battle, besieged on every side by affliction and temptation. Others, after many assaults, repulses, and rallyings of their faith, are already standing upon the wall of heaven as conquerors. From there they look down and urge you, their comrades on earth, to march up the hill after them.

This is their cry: "Fight to the death and the City is your own, as now it is ours! For the waging of a few days' conflict, you will be rewarded with heaven's glory. One moment of this celestial joy will dry up all your tears, heal all your wounds, and erase the sharpness of the fight with the joy of your permanent victory."

In a word – God, angels, and the saints already with the Lord are spectators, watching how you conduct yourself as a child of the Most High. This crowd of witnesses (Hebrews 12:1) shouts joyfully from the celestial sidelines every time you defeat a temptation, scale a difficulty, or regain lost ground from your enemies. And if the fight should be too much for you, your dear Saviour stands by with reserves for your relief at a moment's notice. His very heart leaps with Him to see the proof of your love and zeal for Him in all your combats, He will not forget your faithfulness. And when you come off the field, He will receive you as joyously as the Father received Him upon His return to heaven…[85]

---

[85] Gurnall01, Page 27

Engaged in Battle

As Christians, we are in a battle. We have a great crowd of witnesses urging us on. We march victorious because of the death and resurrection of Jesus Christ, Son of God, our Lord and our Master. Together we wear our armour. We are to grow in grace and in the knowledge of Jesus according to Peter (2 Peter 3:18). This is achieved only through our spending time studying the Bible and seeing what God has to say to us. Then when we hear that nagging little voice that says: "God didn't say that", we can say "Oh yes, He did!"

We are to show total trust in God for our life. The faith we have is a defensive weapon against the mistruths that come into our head: lies, blasphemy, lust, greed, selfishness are all little darts thrown at us by Satan and others. By maintaining our trust in God's promises and God's power, these little darts are extinguished.

We are to be ready to share the Gospel of Jesus Christ with other people and to rely upon it. Because we have peace with God, we are able to withstand without fear the attacks of Satan. We have peace with God, but we are also to exhibit peace with others. Where peace is, the discord of our enemy cannot prevail.

We are to live a life which is honouring to and bringing glory to God by living the truth. When we started as Christians, before God, we were given the righteousness of Jesus. But that righteousness needs to be lived out in our life as Christians. If it isn't, then we can be assured that Satan will attack and accuse.

What's more, is that we can have total assurance of our salvation. We can allow our mind to be controlled by the Holy Spirit, so that we are not led astray. Our salvation rests in nothing apart from God's promises and Jesus' righteousness.

We are to know, understand and live truth. Our life is to be controlled by truth as revealed by the Holy Spirit as we read and study the Bible. When we know truth well, we can recognize the lies that we are being told by other people, inside and outside the Church, as well as the great accuser, the father of lies, who is Satan. We know that with

A Final Word

certainty from events in our past. All these and more, reflect that as Christians, we are clothed in spiritual armour. It is our responsibility to wear it and use it with confidence. We are to be alert to the prowling of Satan and rely solely on God's power to overcome sin and temptation. In our own strength we pretty much always fail, but by using God's strength and remaining clothed in this armour provided by Him, we can be assured that we will prevail and overcome, all to God's praise, honour and glory.

As we prevail in His strength, we show that we are an overcomer who is relying solely upon God. We seek to serve Him wholeheartedly in all aspects of life. Let's go, Church!

Becoming a Christian

If you are not yet a Christian, and you want to turn to God right now, there is no need for delay. He is ready and willing to take you as His own – right now. You only have to ask Him to forgive you and He will! Being a Christian is a partnership between God and yourself. Deciding to change course in mid–life, is what is called conversion, being born again, or deciding to be a Christian. When you place your faith in Jesus, becoming utterly dependent upon Him, you turn to God.

Once you have made that decision, you leave behind your rebellion against Him. As you live each day, becoming more involved with Jesus day by day, you will find yourself changing. You stop doing things which separated you from Him and find yourself doing things that develop your relationship with Him.

How do you develop this relationship? Until you enter into that relationship, sin, or that which alienates you from God, controls your rebellion against Him in your attitudes and your activities. You develop this relationship by allowing God to take control of your life, as He asks you to accept His management and guidance of your life. God's point of view and His strength will become your point of view and your source of strength. You turn your mind, will and heart to Him for all you do. If you want to make that decisive step and become a Christian, there are three simple steps.

Firstly, admit that you have done wrong against God and His ways and turn away from those attitudes.

Secondly, believe and trust in Jesus as your Saviour from the consequences of the anger of God towards you and your tendency to sin. Call on Him, receive, trust, obey and worship Him, recognizing Him for who He is and what He has done.

Thirdly, accept the Holy Spirit of God into your life as the major motivating force for what you do. Once sin has been confessed, Jesus is believed in and trusted as Saviour and the Holy Spirit has entered your

Becoming A Christian

life, then you are a Christian. All these things happen together in a flash as you turn to God. Now you are ready to grow in grace and knowledge of our Jesus.

Welcome to the family of God! God has chosen you; Jesus has paid for you and has put His mark within you through His Spirit (Ephesians 1:1–13).

Chief Abbreviations

à Kempis	The Imitation of Christ, by Thomas à Kempis, Christian Classics Ethereal Library, Grand Rapids, http://www.ccel.org/ccel/kempis/imitation.html
Augustine	On Christian Doctrine, by Augustine, Christian Classics Ethereal Library, Grand Rapids, http://www.ccel.org/ccel/augustine/doctrine.html
Bernard	Loving God, by Bernard of Clairvaux, Christian Classics Ethereal Library, Grand Rapids, http://www.ccel.org/ccel/bernard/loving_god.html
Bonhoeffer	Letters and Papers from Prison, by Dietrich Bonhoeffer, SCM Press, London, 2001
Calvin	The Institutes of the Christian Religion, by John Calvin, Hodder & Stoughton, London, 2006
Carswell	Where Is God In A Messed Up World, by Roger Carswell, 10 Publishing, Leyland, 2020
Christou	Paul & the Unsearchable Riches of Christ, by Sotirios Christou, Phoenix Books, Cambridge, 2006
Chrysostom	Homilies on Galatians, Ephesians, Philippians, Colossians, Thessalonians, Timothy, Titus, and Philemon, by John Chrysostom & PhilipSchaff, Christian Classics Ethereal Library, Grand Rapids, http://www.ccel.org/ccel/schaff/npnf113.html
Drane	Clowns, Storytellers, Disciples, by Olive Drane, The Bible Reading Fellowship, Oxford, 2002
Gurnall01	The Christian in Complete Armour Volume One, by W Gurnall, Banner of Truth Trust, Edinburgh, 1991
Gurnall02	The Christian in Complete Armour Volume Two, by W Gurnall, Banner of Truth Trust, Edinburgh, 1991
Gurnall03	The Christian in Complete Armour Volume Three, by W Gurnall, Banner of Truth Trust, Edinburgh, 1991
Hole	New Testament Commentary: Paul's Epistles Volume 2, by FB Hole, Scripture Truth Publications, Wooler, 1995
Jackman	The Message of John's Letters (Bible Speaks Today series), by David Jackman, IVP, Leicester, 1992

Lennox	Where Is God In A Coronavirus World?, by John C Lennox, The Good Book Company, Epsom, 2020,
Lewis01	Mere Christianity, by CS Lewis, HarperCollins, London, 2002
Lewis02	Surprised by Joy, by CS Lewis, Fount Paperbacks, Glasgow, 1982
Lloyd–Jones01	The Christian Soldier, by DM Lloyd–Jones, Banner of Truth Trust, Edinburgh, 1977
Lloyd–Jones02	Faith on Trial, by DM Lloyd–Jones, IVF, London 1965,
Luther	Table Talk, by Martin Luther, Bridge–Logos, Orlando, 2004
Mann	Naturally Supernatural, by Wendy Mann, Malcolm Down Publishing, 2015,
McGrath	The Journey, by Alister McGrath, Hodder & Stoughton, London, 1999
Moule	Studies in Ephesians, by HCG Moule, Kregel Publications, Grand Rapids, 1977
Olyott	Alive in Christ: Ephesians Simply Explained, by Stuart Olyott, Evangelical Press, Durham, 1994
Skinner	A Comedian's Prayer Book, by F Skinner, Hodder & Stoughton, London, 2021
Stott	The Message of Ephesians: God's New Society. 2nd edition (Bible Speaks Today series), by John RW Stott, IVP, Leicester, 1989
Watson	Discipleship, by David Watson, Hodder & Stoughton, London, 1986
Whitman	Crossway Bible Guide: 1 Peter Free to Hope, by Andrew Whitman, Hodder & Stoughton, London, 1994
Wright	Early Christians Letters for Everyone: James, Peter, John and Judah, by Tom Wright, SPCK, London, 2011

Index of Bible References

OLD TESTAMENT

Genesis 1	81
Genesis 3	18
Genesis 3:24	19
Genesis 18:33	110
Genesis 32:1	20
Genesis 42:16	46
Exodus 3	82
Exodus 3:14–15	94
Exodus 3:15	86
Exodus 4:31	163
Exodus 12:24	86
Exodus 20:1–3	164
Exodus 20:3	89
Exodus 25:17–22	19
Exodus 32	165
Exodus 34	82
Exodus 34:6–7	96
Leviticus 9:23–24	126
Leviticus 11:44–45	97
Numbers 22	82
Deuteronomy 4:20	86
Deuteronomy 6:4	94
Deuteronomy 6:13	89
Deuteronomy 6:16	90
Deuteronomy 8:3	88
Joshua 5:13–15	82
Joshua 10:12–15	95
Judges 2:4	82

1 Samuel 3:3–9	81
1 Samuel 15:22	163
1 Kings 8:46	26
1 Kings 19:5–8	19
2 Kings 19:35	19
1 Chronicles 16:29	163
1 Chronicles 21:16	82
1 Chronicles 29:11	96
Job 1:6	16
Job 2:4–5	16
Job 38:7	18
Psalm 19:2	168
Psalm 22:1–21	68
Psalm 22:22–31	68
Psalm 24:16	69
Psalm 32	26
Psalm 32:5–7	27
Psalm 51	26
Psalm 51:3	31
Psalm 66:1–4	124
Psalm 66:5–12	125
Psalm 66:18	116
Psalm 73	53
Psalm 89:7	19
Psalm 91:11–12	90
Psalm 99:5, 9	163
Psalm 100:4–5	163
Psalm 105:1–7	162
Psalm 119	120
Psalm 133:1–3	153

Psalm 139:1–4............................96
Psalm 139:7–12..........................94
Psalm 147:5................................95
Psalm 148:2–5............................18

Proverbs 6:26.............................57
Proverbs 28:9...........................116

Ecclesiastes 3:11........................82

Isaiah 14:12–15..........................16
Isaiah 59:15–17..........................43

Jeremiah 23:23...........................94
Jeremiah 32:17...........................95

Lamentations 5:19–22............133

Daniel 6:22.................................19
Daniel 10–12..............................19

Habakkuk 3:18........................163

Malachi 3:6.................................95
Malachi 3:8...............................159
Malachi 3:10.............................160
Malachi 3:16–18........................73

Zechariah 1:12...........................82

New Testament
Matthew 2:12.............................82
Matthew 3:1–2...........................31
Matthew 4:1...............................87
Matthew 4:1–11.........................21
Matthew 4:4, 7 & 10..................83
Matthew 4:11.............................19

Matthew 4:17.............................31
Matthew 5:6.............................119
Matthew 5:9.............................147
Matthew 5:11–12.......................73
Matthew 5:13–16.....................146
Matthew 5:17–19.......................83
Matthew 5:20.............................73
Matthew 5:29–30.......................22
Matthew 5:43–48.....................155
Matthew 5:44–48.....................147
Matthew 6:9.............................112
Matthew 6:9–13.......................112
Matthew 7:21...........................143
Matthew 7:21–23.....................142
Matthew 7:21–29............142, 144
Matthew 7:24...........................144
Matthew 7:24–27.....................142
Matthew 7:26...........................144
Matthew 7:29.............................12
Matthew 8:17...........................109
Matthew 8:29–31.......................18
Matthew 10:14–15.....................22
Matthew 10:16...........................60
Matthew 10:28...........................22
Matthew 12:24...........................16
Matthew 12:45...........................18
Matthew 13:19...........................17
Matthew 13:39...........................17
Matthew 14:22–33.....................66
Matthew 14:25...........................69
Matthew 14:29...........................69
Matthew 16:24–27...................149
Matthew 16:27...........................19
Matthew 18:10...........................19
Matthew 19:16–25...................148
Matthew 20:16.........................139
Matthew 20:25–28...................139

179

Matthew 21:28–32	31
Matthew 22:36–40	25
Matthew 25:14–30	157
Matthew 25:34	73
Matthew 25:41	20
Matthew 26:40–41	28
Matthew 26:53	19
Matthew 27:46	74
Matthew 28:5	20
Matthew 28:18–20	19
Mark 1:12	87
Mark 1:15	31
Mark 4:15	16
Mark 5:1–20	18
Mark 6:48	68
Mark 8:38	19
Mark 10:45	60, 62, 156
Mark 12:25	18
Luke 1:11–20	19
Luke 1:26–38	82
Luke 1:37	95
Luke 2:13–14	19
Luke 3:21–23	87
Luke 4:1–2	88
Luke 4:1–13	121
Luke 4:3–4	88
Luke 4:4	88
Luke 4:5–8	89
Luke 4:9–13	90
Luke 6:26	53
Luke 10:18	16
Luke 11:1	112
Luke 12:32–34	74
Luke 13:11, 16	17
Luke 15:7–10	73
Luke 15:10	19
Luke 16:19–25	73
Luke 18:9–14	116
Luke 20:36	18
Luke 22:19	154
Luke 22:19–20	154
Luke 22:31	17
Luke 23:45	106
John 1:16	96
John 3:3	102
John 3:16	97
John 4:23–24	162
John 4:24	94, 96
John 5:24	136
John 8:12	41, 103
John 8:29	88
John 8:34	26
John 8:44	17
John 10:10	49, 132
John 10:10–11	53
John 10:27–29	70
John 10:28–29	20
John 12:31	89
John 12:32	40
John 12:46	103
John 13:34–35	40, 98
John 13:35	153
John 14:1–4	74
John 14:2	73
John 14:6	46, 95, 96, 103
John 14:12	157
John 14:17	158
John 14:30	17
John 15:9–12	103
John 15:16	72
John 15:18–27	34

John 16:11 16
John 16:33 40
John 17 111
John 17:1–3 112
John 17:10 103
John 17:13 129
John 17:14–19 53
John 17:21 65
John 18:4 93

Acts 1:10 20
Acts 2 84
Acts 2:23 100
Acts 2:32 91
Acts 2:38 31
Acts 2:41 84
Acts 2:42 153
Acts 2:42–47 160
Acts 4:18–20 37
Acts 4:32–36 160
Acts 15:14 65
Acts 17:30 31
Acts 18:2, 7–8 & 17 61
Acts 18:3, 4 & 11 61
Acts 18:3, 13 60
Acts 18:4, 6 60
Acts 18:6 61
Acts 18:7 61
Acts 19:13 18
Acts 20:21 31
Acts 21 36

Romans 1:18–25 167
Romans 2:8–9 22
Romans 3:20 31
Romans 3:21–26 52
Romans 3:23 26

Romans 4:24–25 92
Romans 5:1 .... 92, 106
Romans 5:1b, 10 107
Romans 5:2 106
Romans 5:3–4 106
Romans 5:5–8 107
Romans 5:9–10 107
Romans 5:10 .... 92, 103
Romans 5:11 107
Romans 6:1–23 153
Romans 6:4 24
Romans 6:6 24
Romans 6:6, 11 &14 29
Romans 6:19–20 26
Romans 7:15–8:3 29
Romans 8:7 29
Romans 8:10 92
Romans 8:17–18 73
Romans 8:22–25 75
Romans 8:26 111
Romans 8:28 .... 106, 135
Romans 8:28–29 .... 48, 132
Romans 8:34 68
Romans 8:38–39 70
Romans 9 72
Romans 10:8–11 143
Romans 10:9 58
Romans 11:33 .... 95, 96
Romans 12:1 .... 119, 163
Romans 12:2 .... 163, 164
Romans 12:6 158
Romans 12:6–8 .... 158, 159
Romans 13 37
Romans 13:1–7 35
Romans 14:22–23 54
Romans 15:25–27 108
Romans 15:30–32 87

181

Romans 15:7 153

1 Corinthians 1:9 153
1 Corinthians 2 105
1 Corinthians 2:1–5 58
1 Corinthians 2:2 .... 58, 61
1 Corinthians 5:12 63
1 Corinthians 6:3 .... 18, 20
1 Corinthians 7:1–5 40
1 Corinthians 8:6 94
1 Corinthians 8:9–13 54
1 Corinthians 9:19–23 108
1 Corinthians 10:12–13 ..... 28, 30
1 Corinthians 10:14–21 108
1 Corinthians 10:16 154
1 Corinthians 10:17 154
1 Corinthians 10:23–24 54
1 Corinthians 10:31 54
1 Corinthians 11:24 154
1 Corinthians 11:25 154
1 Corinthians 11:26 154
1 Corinthians 11:28–29 154
1 Corinthians 12:3 143
1 Corinthians 12:7 158
1 Corinthians 12:8–10 158
1 Corinthians 12:11 158
1 Corinthians 12:28–30 158
1 Corinthians 13:12 111
1 Corinthians 14:1–12 159
1 Corinthians 14:12 158
1 Corinthians 14:26 165
1 Corinthians 15:12–58 92
1 Corinthians 15:57 153
1 Corinthians 16:2 159

2 Corinthians 1:6–7 108
2 Corinthians 1:8 69

2 Corinthians 2:11 .... 17, 91
2 Corinthians 3:18 .... 48, 132
2 Corinthians 4:4 17
2 Corinthians 4:7–9 138
2 Corinthians 4:14 92
2 Corinthians 5:2–8 74
2 Corinthians 5:14 63
2 Corinthians 5:17 102
2 Corinthians 5:20 25
2 Corinthians 7:8–10 31
2 Corinthians 8:1–15 153
2 Corinthians 8:4 153
2 Corinthians 9:7 159
2 Corinthians 11:3 17
2 Corinthians 11:14 30
2 Corinthians 11:14–15 17
2 Corinthians 12:2–4 73

Galatians 2:5 46
Galatians 2:9 153
Galatians 4:4–7 103
Galatians 5:16 29
Galatians 5:19–21 29
Galatians 5:22–23 76
Galatians 5:22–25 47

Ephesians 1:1–13 175
Ephesians 1:5–7 103
Ephesians 1:13 46
Ephesians 2:2 17
Ephesians 2:3 29
Ephesians 2:3–5 96
Ephesians 2:5 102
Ephesians 2:7 96
Ephesians 2:8–10 63
Ephesians 2:10 100
Ephesians 2:14 106

Ephesians 3:8–11 100	Colossians 2:15 20
Ephesians 2:22 103	Colossians 2:18 20
Ephesians 4:11 158	Colossians 3:24 .... 163, 164
Ephesians 4:11–16 153	
Ephesians 4:12 158	1 Thessalonians 2:18 30
Ephesians 4:14 134	1 Thessalonians 3:5 17
Ephesians 4:22–24 24	1 Thessalonians 5:22 54
Ephesians 4:23 104	1 Thessalonians 5:23 56
Ephesians 4:24 102	1 Thessalonians 5:25 87
Ephesians 4:27 91	
Ephesians 4:31 21	2 Thessalonians 1:9 22
Ephesians 4:32 40	
Ephesians 5:8 103	1 Timothy 1:3 120
Ephesians 6:10 .... 15, 94	1 Timothy 1:16 95
Ephesians 6:10–17 .... 30, 42, 91	1 Timothy 2:1–3 36
Ephesians 6:11 .... 17, 91	1 Timothy 2:3–4 72
Ephesians 6:12 17	1 Timothy 2:4 31
Ephesians 6:16 17	1 Timothy 4:1 17
Ephesians 6:18–20 .... 87, 110	1 Timothy 4:11–12 139
	1 Timothy 4:14 159
Philippians 1:3–6 153	1 Timothy 6:3–4 120
Philippians 1:3–7 108	1 Timothy 6:15–16 96
Philippians 1:5 153	1 Timothy 6:20 139
Philippians 1:6 70	
Philippians 2:1 153	2 Timothy 2:19 70
Philippians 2:3 40	2 Timothy 3:16 82
Philippians 2:12–13 72	2 Timothy 3:16–17 .... 48, 122
Philippians 3:10 153	2 Timothy 4:3 118
Philippians 3:12–14 136	2 Timothy 4:5 63
Philippians 3:20–21 56	2 Timothy 4:10 29
Philippians 4:3 73	
Philippians 4:12–13 138	Titus 1:9 120
Philippians 4:19 160	Titus 3:5 102
Colossians 1:3–5 152	Hebrews 1:13–14 18
Colossians 1:15–20 11	Hebrews 1:14 .... 18, 19
Colossians 1:18 12	Hebrews 2:14 .... 17, 20

Hebrews 2:14–18	108
Hebrews 4:14–16	68
Hebrews 4:15	26
Hebrews 6:20	92
Hebrews 7:26	97
Hebrews 10:19–25	152
Hebrews 10:24–25	153
Hebrews 11:6	68
Hebrews 11:39–40	153
Hebrews 12:1	171
Hebrews 12:1–2	139
Hebrews 12:1–3	136
Hebrews 12:10–11	108
Hebrews 13:2	20
Hebrews 13:8	95
James 1:2–4	135
James 1:5–7	116
James 1:8	134
James 1:14–15	91
James 3:15	17
James 4:3	116
James 4:4	29
James 4:7	21, 91
James 4:17	26
James 5:16	134, 153
1 Peter 1:3, 21	92
1 Peter 1:4	73
1 Peter 1:5	70
1 Peter 1:10–12	83
1 Peter 1:15	97
1 Peter 1:21	92
1 Peter 2:13–17	36
1 Peter 3:12	69
1 Peter 4:10	157
1 Peter 4:11	158

1 Peter 4:12–13	108
1 Peter 4:12–14	54
1 Peter 4:16	135
1 Peter 5:1–4	108
1 Peter 5:8	17, 30, 161
1 Peter 5:9	20, 30, 91
2 Peter 1:1–4	108
2 Peter 1:4	29
2 Peter 1:19–20	83
2 Peter 2:4	16, 18, 22
2 Peter 3:9	31, 72
2 Peter 3:13	73, 74
2 Peter 3:15–16	83
2 Peter 3:18	80, 172
1 John 1:3	153
1 John 1:7	26, 152, 153
1 John 1:8–10	27
1 John 1:9	21
1 John 1:10	27
1 John 2:3–6	103
1 John 2:15	29
1 John 2:15–17	29
1 John 2:16	28
1 John 3:6	26
1 John 3:8	20
1 John 3:20	95
1 John 4:1	29
1 John 4:1–3	46, 47
1 John 4:4	20, 30
1 John 4:4–5	21
1 John 4:7–9	97
1 John 4:8–10	96
1 John 4:11	153
1 John 4:16	81, 97
1 John 4:20	155

1 John 5:1–5 104
1 John 5:4 153
1 John 5:6–12 62
1 John 5:18 .... 20, 25
1 John 5:19 .... 17, 28

2 John 7 29

Jude 6 16
Jude 9 19

Revelation 2–3......................... 19
Revelation 4:11...................... 163
Revelation 5:11........................ 18
Revelation 5:11–12.................. 19
Revelation 7:15........................ 73
Revelation 12:7........................ 16
Revelation 12:7–10.................. 77
Revelation 12:9........................ 16
Revelation 12:10................ 17, 30
Revelation 13:8........................ 22
Revelation 14:11...................... 22
Revelation 14:13...................... 73
Revelation 19:8........................ 73
Revelation 19:20...................... 22
Revelation 21:1.................. 26, 75
Revelation 21:1–4.................... 74
Revelation 21:2........................ 73
Revelation 21:6........................ 94
Revelation 21:8........................ 22
Revelation 20:10...................... 16
Revelation 20:12................ 22, 73
Revelation 21:21...................... 73
Revelation 22:8–9.................... 20
Revelation 22:9........................ 20
Revelation 22:14...................... 73
Revelation 22:20...................... 78

Other PulpTheology Publications

AGOG: A Glimpse of God
An Ambassador in God's Orchestra of Joy
Dear Christian – Get A Good Grip
Dear Church: Wake up!
Developing Intimacy With God: A Little Book of 95 Prayers
Easter Essentials: Exploring Easter
Exploring The Bible
God Gets His Hands Dirty
God, Internet Church & You
God's Two Words For You: Jesus and the Bible.
Helping the Forgotten Church
Heroes And Heretics Abound – History of the Church
Intimacy with God: The Christian Devotional Life
Living Life Right: Studies in Romans 12
Scriptural Delights: Exploring Psalm 119
When Love Hits Town
WOW Words of the Bible

WHAT'S IT ALL ABOUT ALPHY SERIES

The Lord's Prayer
The Surprise of Grace (Romans 5)
The Christian In Days Of Challenge (Romans 8)

Glimpses Into Series:

Leviticus: A Book Of Joy
1 & 2 Chronicles: Books of heritage And history
Psalms: A Book Of Life
Song Of Songs: A Book Of Relationship
Ezekiel: A Book Of Symbols And Visions
The Gospels: Books Of Good News
Acts: A Book Of Action
Romans: A Book Of Freedom

Read This Book Series:

Volume 1: God Of The Bible
Volume 2: Jesus Christ
Volume 3: Being Christians
Volume 4: The Church
Volume 5: Evangelism
Volume 6: The Christian Devotional Life

All books are available in Paperback and Kindle at:
PulpTheology.co.uk
PulpTheology.com
And all Amazon sites

About Partakers

Vision Statement: Partakers exists to communicate and distribute resources for the purposes of Christian discipleship, Evangelism and Worship by employing radical and relevant methods, including virtual reality and online distribution.

Mission Statement: To help the world, one person at a time, to engage in whole life discipleship, as Partakers of Jesus Christ.

Contact us to see how we can help you. Seminars, coaching, preaching, teaching, discipleship or evangelism – offline or online.

Email: dave@partakers.co.uk
Mobile: 0794 794 5511
Website: http://www.partakers.co.uk

Printed in Poland
by Amazon Fulfillment
Poland Sp. z o.o., Wrocław
12 November 2022

1b7aeb84-301e-4383-bcdb-5c64c3e5cf03R01